I'D TRADE
MY HUSBAND
for a
HOUSEKEEPER

I'D TRADE MY HUSBAND *for a* HOUSEKEEPER

loving your marriage *after* the baby carriage

TRISHA ASHWORTH *and* AMY NOBILE

CHRONICLE BOOKS
SAN FRANCISCO

Manufactured in Canada
Design by Jennifer Tolo Pierce
Typesetting by Janis Reed

Library of Congress Cataloging-in-Publication Data
Ashworth, Trisha.
  I'd trade my husband for a housekeeper : loving your marriage
after the baby carriage / Trisha Ashworth and Amy Nobile.
      p. cm.
  ISBN 978-0-8118-6735-1
 1. Marriage. 2. Sex in marriage. 3. Communication in marriage.
4. Man-woman relationships. I. Nobile, Amy. II. Title. III. Title:
I would trade my husband for a housekeeper.
  HQ734.A74 2009
  646.7'8—dc22
2008032464

10 9 8 7 6 5 4 3 2 1

Chronicle Books
680 Second Street
San Francisco, California 94107
www.chroniclebooks.com

www.reallygoodmom.com
Some names in this book have been changed.

for Eric and Paul,
Your love and laughter is the inspiration for everything else.

CONTENTS

CHAPTER 1

BEYOND
the
BITCH SESSION

(Why We Wrote This Book)

quiz *no. 1*

You need this book if . . .

Check all that apply:

☐ You spend more time with Mr. Potato Head than your husband.

☐ You're psyched when your husband goes on a business trip because you won't have to shave your legs.

☐ You think sex is something people do on soap operas.

☐ You're green with envy upon hearing that your best friend's hubby knows how to sew on a button.

☐ You've fantasized about spraining your ankle just so you can spend some quiet hours alone in the emergency room.

☐ Your last "date night" was . . . when you were dating.

☐ You consider your five-year-old to be more mature than your husband because your five-year-old knows how to clean his room.

☐ You wonder what the FedEx guy does for "fun."

- [ ] You fondly remember the days when your biggest stress was buying the right tampons.

- [ ] Your husband's idea of a great day with the kids is going to the hardware store and then to Best Buy to check out the new plasma TVs.

- [ ] You spy on your husband doing the dishes because it turns you on.

- [ ] Your bras can stand up and walk away on their own.

- [ ] You find yourself asking your preschool daughter if her daddy ever says nice things about you.

- [ ] You rationalize not washing your hair for another day because it will save you twenty minutes.

- [ ] Getting ready to go to an amusement park with the family might throw you into divorce court.

- [ ] The last time you wore a sexy nightgown—let alone lingerie—was on your honeymoon.

- [ ] Your husband knows every major league baseball player's batting average but doesn't know your kids' teachers' names.

If there's one thing MORE TABOO

THAN ADMITTING YOU'RE A TRAIN WRECK OF A MOTHER,

IT'S SAYING YOU THINK YOUR MARRIAGE IS RUNNING OFF

the rails. We're not talking about a little good old-fashioned bitching, like when you're in a bad mood and you tell your girlfriend at the grocery store that if your husband doesn't start forming a more intimate relationship with the bathroom hamper, you're thinking of forming an intimate relationship with someone else. Sounding off like that is acceptable, cathartic—a normal part of life. What's hard—and not so acceptable—is making an honest, gut-wrenching assessment of the honest, gut-wrenching state of your marriage. Particularly if you're in a marriage that involves kids.

Let's face it: Kids, god bless 'em, are a marriage bomb. You pop one out and—wham!—your whole relationship is scrambled like an omelet. Your family role is now split: One minute you're a wife, the next you're a mom (though most of the time you're expected to be both). The stress level in your house explodes. Too tired to make dinner, too frenzied to communicate, too wrung-out by the under-sized darlings clinging to your hands, legs, and boobs to have any interest in clinging to the big darling beside you in bed, the seeds of resentment take root, and quickly bloom.

We explored this a little in our first book, *I Was a Really Good Mom Before I Had Kids*. In our research we talked to hundreds of moms coast-to-coast—single moms, working moms, stay-at-home moms—and found that one of the biggest issues on mothers' minds today is how parenthood affects our relationships with our spouses. "Before kids, he used to come home from work and give me a hug. Now he walks in the door and immediately says, 'OK! Everybody needs to calm down! Everybody needs to lower their voices!' Are you *kidding* me?" one mother of three told us. Of course, some mothers have happier marriages than others. One lucky mama told us, "My husband's mantra is 'Happy Wife, Happy Life.' He can clue into what makes me happy and support that." But for each cooing mother we talked to, we heard from one (or two, or three) who were losing their minds. "I don't know how to ask for help. I just know how to scream at my husband," was a familiar refrain.

What we learned from our interviews was that the pressures and challenges of modern motherhood have created a new set of obstacles for married couples today.

We thought we'd deal with this by writing a nice long chapter about husbands and leave it at that. Yet once *I Was a Really Good Mom Before I Had Kids* came out, we started getting stopped on the street by women who'd read the husband chapter and said it really resonated with them. They asked us for more. More quotes from more women about what their marriages are really like. More discussion about why kids seem so incompatible with conjugal bliss. More about

DIRTY LITTLE SECRET

If I could pay someone to have sex for me, I would!

how the stresses and uncertainties facing contemporary mothers are permeating all aspects of our lives. We got e-mails and letters from women all saying the same thing—"I just read your husband chapter. I've been needing that! Please write more." We also heard from husbands, including one who said, "Thank you [words we're always happy to hear out of a man's mouth]! My wife made me read your book, and it really helped us understand each other a little better."

We even heard from our own husbands, Eric and Paul. One night at a dinner party, they discussed the book they'd write if they had the chance. The table of contents:

Chapter One:	Stop Yelling at Me
Chapter Two:	Don't Be Mean to Me
Chapter Three:	What Do I Have to Do to Get You to Take Off Your Clothes? Because I'll Do It.

Ouch! Guess we needed to write this book more than we realized! Have we been yelling? We're certainly not mean . . . are we? And as far as sex goes . . . well, OK, they may have a point (we'll talk more about that later). Still, their (ahem!) experience of marriage convinced us even more that we needed to dig deeper into the male perspective—to find out what husbands expected, what they think is working, what they really wish could change. If we don't understand where our husbands are coming from, and they don't understand where we're coming from, we can't possibly get to that happy place in marriage where we all hope to be!

You can see how it all panned out. After enough people reached out to us, we decided to go for it and get back to work. First, we started asking ourselves questions about marriage, and then we took those questions on the road (or to the telephone, as was often the case). We interviewed hundreds of married women (and many men), all of them parents. We asked: What happened to your marriage after you had kids? Why did you get married in the first place? Do you think it's harder to be happily married today? What specific challenges in your life right now are preventing you from being completely satisfied or fulfilled? Are you happy?

Many of these questions were met with silence . . . followed by emotional answers. It was clear in those silences that talking about what's really going on inside a marriage feels taboo and scary. We've all made an implicit pact with our friends and families that aside from a little superficial bitching, the true problems of our marriages will be swept under the rug. When you get beyond the bitching, we learned, most of us immediately start worrying that (a) people will think we're crazy, and (b) the state of our marriages will be judged. We've all got social and conversational comfort zones, and as our interviews started inching toward those hard "dealbreaker" conversations—discussions about the things that can actually lead couples toward divorce—people immediately fell out of those comfort zones.

We even learned some things about our own marriages in the process—like that it's outside the bounds of regulation marriage play to have relationship books lying around the house. One evening Paul, Amy's husband, cornered her in a cold sweat. He'd seen the pile of research books on her bedside table. "Are we OK? Is there something you want to talk about?" he asked her once the kids were finally down and they were very romantically flossing their teeth together. (Guess he kind of forgot we were writing this book!)

Yet here's the interesting part—and something we should have expected after working on the motherhood book but still didn't quite see coming: Once the wives and husbands we interviewed decided to take a leap of faith and trust us, the floodgates opened. One woman we interviewed tearfully confessed for the first time—to us—that her husband had been having an affair and she was contemplating divorce. She told us this while on the phone at work, shuttling from one conference room to the next, as various meetings started. We found that after wives got over the feeling that they were weird, lame, or both for finding marriage difficult, they put aside their fears, and we got down to the nitty-gritty of what's really going on in people's marriages.

We started out by asking some fairly simple questions:

- Why do we put our marriages last on the priority list?

- Why do we put so much pressure on ourselves as mothers today?

- What happened to our sex lives?

- Why are our marriages—after kids—not all that we expected them to be?

- What happened to the person we were before we became "Mom"?

- Why does communication (and appreciation) seem like so much of a struggle now that we have kids?

- Why can't we talk about marriage openly and honestly with other people (and why do other marriages seem more "together" than ours)?

We want to be clear here: This isn't a desperate housewives book. If you've just plain married the wrong person, there's not much this book can do for you. But if you think you've married the right person, and your marriage isn't all it could be, this is for you. Most of the women and men we spoke to rated themselves at about a 5 or 6 on a 10-point happiness scale. Not so bad, not so good . . . just kind of, you know, cruising, and hoping that once the kids are older or out of the house they'll fall back in love.

A lot of our conversations went like this:

Us: *How would you rate your marriage on a scale of 1 to 10?*

Them: Uh . . . *hmmm*. . . a 5? Maybe a 6?

Us: *Are you OK with that?*

Them: No, definitely not.

Us: *So how do you plan on getting from a 5 to a 10?*

[Long silence]

Them: Well, I'm assuming we'll just get happier, right? Maybe next year? When the kids get older?

We can't tell you how many long silences we heard over the past year, and we came to grow oddly fond of them. "Where does your husband fall on your priority list?" Silence. "What do you think would make your marriage work better?" Silence. Most of these silences were followed by something like, "Wow, I've never actually thought about that." You could almost hear people's brains churning. Many of us have not asked ourselves some really important questions about our marriages—like, for starters: "How can I be more proactive about having a happier marriage?" And once you put a question like that out there, it's nearly impossible to take it back.

Oftentimes our interviews turned into ad hoc therapy sessions, even when we were calling marriage counselors to get data or advice. We'd like to think it's because we asked such brilliant questions, but the truth is that people opened up to us because they wanted to and needed to, and because they have so few chances to do so. It's hard to talk about marriage with people you know. Nobody wants to be given sideways glances at a dinner party, not even a couples counselor. So, we'd call up therapists for stats and come away with another marriage confession from another mom.

Here are some of the things we heard:

- The high expectations we have of ourselves to be a "good mom" supercede those of being a "good wife."

- The pressure to be a "good mom" leaves little room for relationships, and as a result our marriages end up way down on our priority lists.

- We could be happier in our marriages, but we're not sure how to get there.

- We know nobody has a perfect marriage, but we can't help thinking the fantasy ideal exists anyway.

- Having a happy sex life is much harder after having kids.

- We've put our marriages on cruise control, without any real plan as to how to take charge of our relationships again, short of waiting for the kids to grow up.

This book has a few different goals—all of them aimed at helping you love being married to your husband (as much as you did before you had kids). First, we want to give women permission to make their relationship a priority (without feeling selfish or guilty). Second, we want to help women understand what their husbands are going through as well. (The challenges facing a modern-day husband and father are huge, coupled with the fact that men often don't talk about their feelings like women do.) Third, we want women to gain insight into who *they* are, and who *he* is, to remember why they got married in the first place, and what this whole messy family thing is for.

We're all so busy, and it's so easy to focus on all the little things that are wrong, that many of us lose perspective altogether. Socks left on the floor can drive us to the breaking point. Getting home a half hour late can set off a marital disaster. With this book we're hoping to offer relief and optimism, to put things into context and perspective. We want to empower women to start focusing on the bigger picture, lest we fall into those horrid divorce statistics. What do you want your marriage to look like in one year? In five years? What can you do today to work toward that? A good marriage requires a steadfast intention to keep it on track. Of course every marriage is different, and every day can throw up huge obstacles to a blissful union. But if we pay close attention—hell, if we pay half the attention to our spouses that we do to our kids—we'll all be a lot happier than we are now.

Nearly every divorce lawyer we spoke to told us the same thing—that many of their clients could have saved their marriages if they'd only actively worked on their problems before they escalated. Which brings us back to all of us who are complacently lingering at 5 or 6 on the marriage happiness scale, assuming we'll bounce back up to 8 or 9 once the kids leave the house. At what point did we decide it was okay to just feel OK about our marriages? Here we are, a generation of successful women who can take control—occasionally too much control—of every aspect of our lives, and we're choosing to have marriages that we aren't completely happy with. We're choosing to miss out on a great piece of happiness, and that's a shame.

One day, a woman bitched to us, "I'd trade my husband for a housekeeper." We all laughed a great, knowing laugh. But then we took the time to really picture spending our lives with a housekeeper instead of the guy we married. That image wasn't pretty. So we decided to dig a little deeper. This book is what we found.

DIRTY LITTLE SECRET

I liked me more before we had kids, so I liked him more.

(not so) easy steps
to a happier marriage

1.   Know that there's no such thing as a perfect marriage. Stop focusing on what you think your marriage *should* look like and start thinking about what will actually make you happy. There's no set formula for a good marriage. At least half the job is figuring out what a "good marriage" means for you and your spouse in particular. Are your expectations for your spouse and your marriage realistic?

2.   Give yourself permission to make your marriage a priority. The pressures of being a "good mom" in this generation have put our marriages last on our lists.

3.   Commit yourself to working at being happy, instead of waiting for happiness to fall out of the sky. Define your goals together, for both the short and long term. Happiness builds on itself.

CHAPTER 2

WHY DON'T WE HAVE  HOLLYWOOD MARRIAGES?

• • •

(Expectations vs. Reality)

quiz *no. 2*

Did you ever expect that . . .

Check all that apply:

☐ Being a "good mom" would always override being a "good wife"?

☐ You would spend the rest of your life worrying about your kids?

☐ You'd be scheduling sex with your husband?

☐ You'd refer to your husband as "Daddy"?

☐ You'd be more concerned with making sure your kid is wearing the right soccer uniform than whether there's any food in the fridge for your husband?

☐ You'd yell at your kids? And your husband? And the dog?

☐ You would never again be able to stay awake to see the end of a movie?

☐ Your ass would be the size of a double-wide?

☐ Watching your kids grow up, learn to read, adopt family expressions and gestures, and play independently with each other would be so completely amazing?

- [ ] You'd keep a "who does more housework" tally in your head?

- [ ] You'd feel guilty for not feeding your kids organic meals?

- [ ] You'd lose your sex drive?

- [ ] You'd have an uncontrollable fondness for sweatpants, yoga pants, or any pants with an elastic waistband?

- [ ] Homework would be on *your* to-do list?

- [ ] You'd feel guilty getting a pedicure, yet your husband would feel fine about taking off for three hours to play hoops with his buddies?

- [ ] It would require so much conscious effort to schedule a night out with your husband every once in a while?

- [ ] You'd be so touched seeing your husband read bedtime stories to your kids?

We realize that YOU MIGHT NOT BE
IN DIRE CRISIS MODE IN YOUR MARRIAGE RIGHT NOW, BUT
IF YOU'RE LIKE MOST WOMEN, YOU PROBABLY COULD BE
happier. In fact, of more than 300 married women with kids we interviewed, 240 said they could be happier. And nearly all thought they
were in the minority in their feelings. What's more, they thought their
unhappiness was their fault.

But after talking—and talking, and talking—to so many women,
we noticed a trend: Of the 80 percent of women who wished they
were happier in marriage, most started out with an unrealistic vision
of what married life would look like. Particularly married life with
kids. As we wrote in our first book, when our expectations aren't
met, unhappiness ensues. Never mind that our expectations were
unrealistic in the first place and were never going to happen in a mil-
lion years. We had a vision. We didn't attain it. We feel like we failed.

Which leads us to the big question: Why are so many of us in
this situation? While we can blame our parents, Hollywood movies,
celebrity culture, the insidious development of the BlackBerry, the
truth is we're all complicit. We tend to blow a lot of sunshine up
other people's skirts. We tell our friends and coworkers how much

we love being mothers, and put a pretty good varnish on our marriages as well. "I had heard a lot of girlfriends talk about how you fall in love all over again with your husband after you have a baby," one mom named Christy told us. "How you're on cloud nine 24 hours a day. And I kept waiting for that moment to come—more of that 'over the moon' feeling, when you just stare at your husband and say, 'Wow!' But I just didn't have that."

Sister, between the sleeplessness, spit-up, sore boobs, and constant screaming, who could possibly have that?

We're not sharing this so we can all shed a big tear of pity for ourselves. We're sharing this to open each other's eyes. How's anybody supposed to feel satisfied with their marriage, or even know what a good marriage looks like, if we don't talk about marriage and motherhood openly and honestly? As one mom told us, "I didn't talk to anyone about how we were having a hard time—not even my work friends. It's an image thing. I wanted the world to think of me as a working married mom with a great family. It was painful—I knew that wasn't how my life was."

"People are actually less happy today than in the prior generation," Joshua Coleman, Ph.D., author of *The Lazy Husband*, explains. "The first problem is expectations. Today we expect our partner to be everything to us. Our workout partner, our coach, our lover, our friend." The next problem, Dr. Coleman says, is that we tend to enter into marriage with ludicrously overblown notions of what it will be like. We think we'll have perfect communication; star-aligned value systems; great sex after kids; the perfect house; a long-lasting, healthy, best-friendship marriage . . . the list goes on and on. And while that's all really nice, we need to get those visions out of our heads and start talking realistically about marriage if we want to be happy in it. Marriage and motherhood are difficult—but they can also be magical and worthwhile. Counterintuitive as it may seem,

we've got to start acknowledging real marriage—flawed marriage—
if we want to learn to enjoy the marriages we've got.

"I never said one word when we were going through the hard times in our marriage. If I said it out loud, then it was real. But as long as I didn't admit it out loud, then I didn't really have to admit it to myself."

NANCY, married 12 years, 2 children, Keego Harbor, MI

I THOUGHT WE'D COOK DINNER TOGETHER WHILE GIGGLING ABOUT OUR DAY

When we asked women about their expectations going into marriage,
particularly expectations relative to marriage with kids, here is what
we heard:

- Once we have kids, our roles will be interchangeable.

- We will have a 50-50 division of labor.

- We'll make all of our decisions together.

- We'll be even closer after we have kids.

- We'll cook dinner together while giggling about our day.

- We might go through a rough patch sex-wise with the new baby, but we'll get back to "normal" in no time.

- We will always take care of each other—mind, body, and soul.

- My husband stayed the same guy when we got married; he'll stay the same after we have kids.

- We'll adjust our lives to support each other's goals.

- My husband knows me really well; he'll pitch in when he sees I'm tired.

- We'll talk openly and honestly about everything.

- We'll have a lot of family time together.

- Even if life at home gets stressful, our family vacations will be relaxing and fun.

Compounding the problem, many of us assumed our husbands had these same rosy expectations of marriage. In reality, many did not. As Bill, a father of two daughters, told us, "I have two little girls, and their favorite stories are about princesses getting married! Guys have a much less romantic view of marriage. When guys talk about marriage, we buy into this idea of 'giving things up.' We're doing our duty. We go into [marriage] automatically thinking the romance is out of it. And I didn't know it at first. It was a running joke: 'Welcome to the team,' and all that. Your pals make fun of you and tell you what it's really like. And later on you go, 'Oh, you meant it?' It's *tough*—it's a lot of work! Guys expect to work. This is just another form of work."

Women, however, tend to think that finding the right person is the hard part of getting married, not the beginning of a life's work. As Dr. Pat Covalt, author of *What Smart Couples Know*, explained to us, "I think what happens is we women are totally unrealistic about love and romance in marriage. We get caught up more in the gown that we're going to wear than what our conflict management style is." The *in love* feeling women focus on can also lead to trouble down the road. "I don't even use the words 'fall in love' anymore," Covalt says. "Love dissipates. The romantic, jittery stuff—that 'in love' feeling—always goes away, [followed by] a mature level of love that is much less exciting but much more real. People say, 'I love you, but I'm not *in love* with you, so I'll end the marriage.' We need to grow up and be more mature in [our] expectations of marriage. *You should be this sweet little thing you always were.* . . Well, I'm too tired to be sweet—I'm going to bed!"

"I thought as a family we'd all hang out all the time, read books, play Monopoly. Now with working, there's no time to mess around. *Bam, bam, bam*—dinner's on the table, bath time, half-hour TV, read books, go to bed. We're like robots."

SARA, married 10 years, 2 children, Bucks County, PA

I DON'T FEEL LIKE I'M IN LOVE, WITH DOVES FLYING OVER MY HEAD

Of course, in hindsight it's easy to see how idealistic this all was. Falling in love is temporary insanity. And then you come back to your senses and you're left with toothpaste all over the sink, a husband glued to the couch watching hoops for the entirety of March, and old buddies of his who come over and eat all your food. To put it another way, women wake up from falling in love to the realization that life is not one big romance. For men, that waking up often means accepting that the mother of your children doesn't have sex on the forefront of her mind after a long day of getting pelted with Cheerios.

As we discussed in our first book, parenting seldom turns out exactly as we had imagined. The same is true for marriage. "I don't feel like I'm in love, with the doves flying over my head and my heart skipping beats and all that," one mom explained. "Sometimes when I'm angry at him I think, 'Well, is it really supposed to be that way? Am I not feeling "in love" with him?' When I'm not angry I think, 'Maybe I really am in love with him,' but I never know if my feelings are true."

We've learned from our research that one of the main ingredients of a happy marriage is a shared, realistic vision of what that marriage is. As well as explicitly discussing what you each expect and the best way to get there. The men we're married to are husbands and fathers in their own idiosyncratic ways. We can't change them—not the bad singing to the car radio, not the way he likes to eat chicken breasts without using a fork—but we can change the pictures we carry around in our heads of what our unions are supposed to look like. Just connecting with each other, on a daily or even weekly basis, about the joys and difficulties in our days, about how we're feeling as parents, can be a huge relief and pave the road for success. Do you think he expects you to stay home with the kids? Have you asked him? Does he know that the reason you're so mad is that you've been waiting for him to get up with the baby in the middle of the night? Does he know that you're always wearing shorts and running shoes at 5:45 p.m. because you want to go for a jog when he gets home from work? Have you talked about working out a schedule? Have you told him how fantastically turned-on you'll be if he even offers to help you change the sheets?

DIRTY LITTLE SECRET

My husband said, "Maybe you'll stop snoring when you lose the baby weight."

"We had conversations about kids. I was like, *This is so great, we have exactly the same value systems—how is this possible?* And then we had kids, and the verbiage coming out of his mouth . . . I couldn't believe it! Just the other night Charlie was rocking back in his chair, and my husband gave him this little dope slap on the back of his head, and I was just appalled!"

LILLY, married 12 years, 2 children, Scottsdale, AZ

"I struggle with the 'good mom' thing, but I accept that as my role. He doesn't expect a hot dinner every night. But I have that expectation of myself—if I'm a stay-at-home mom and my mom did it, then I should be able to do it, too."

MELISSA, married 9½ years, 4 children, Concord, MA

ARE WE DONE YET?

• • •

In most marriages, at some point, it becomes a big bone of contention: Are we going to have more kids?

It's a huge decision, of course, and most people bring mountains of baggage to the discussion. Many moms and dads we talked to said they had an image in their heads of what their families would look like, including how many kids they'd have. So it really helps to take the time to ask each other some critical questions in order to make more conscious choices about your families. Remember, make the choice that's best for you; we're all going to have different answers to these questions.

- *Why* do we want more children?

- Do we both feel the same way about it?

- What are we looking for in having another child?

- How will having another child affect our current children?

- How will having another child affect our marriage?

- How will having another child affect our finances—both short term and long term? (Consider everything from vacations to schooling to housing needs to childcare.)

- Where do I fit in this? Will I be able to maintain my identity and sanity?

- Will having another child make us happier? Will we be happy without another child?

It's also important to be really honest with yourself about whether "good mom" pressures are coloring your decision-making process. It's crazy, but many of us have had to consider whether we thought having another child would make us look like more successful moms.

At the same time, we need to validate the idea that preserving and nurturing a marriage is a sound, smart reason to *not* have more kids. As one husband named Ben told his wife who was pressuring him to have a third child, "Don't think about it as not having another child . . . think about it as gaining a husband."

Finally, remember that *you* have to live with your choices, and no one else outside your family cares how many kids you have. Whether you have one child or four, make a choice that's right for you and your spouse. Life is full of serendipity and surprise anyway. So plan to have the number of kids that seems best for you.

I ALMOST KILLED MYSELF BAKING MY CHILD'S BIRTHDAY CAKE

In order to understand the pressures we feel in our marriage, we need to first look at the pressures we feel as mothers today.

While researching our first book, we interviewed over a hundred moms nationwide and found a startlingly common thread: their expectations of themselves were over the top. Most moms are carrying this idea of the "good mom" that's completely unrealistic. And as a result, we had a lot of conversations that went like this:

Us: *Tell us a little something about yourself.*

Them: Well, I'm thirty-six, I have two kids, and I used to be a manager of a pharmaceutical company. I finally got a big promotion right before I had my first child.

Us: *How are you handling motherhood right now?*

Them: It's amazing. I love it! I am so balanced. My husband is my *best* friend. I feel *really* blessed and *extremely* lucky that I have healthy kids and we're able to provide a great foundation and a positive environment for our children.

TWENTY-TWO MINUTES LATER:

Us: *Sounds like you have real balance in your life. A lot of women we've talked to seem to have a hard time finding that. How do you do it?*

Them: Ummm, well, maybe "balance" isn't the right word. *[Long pause.]* Umm, actually, I haven't taken a shower in three days. And, OK, my husband and I haven't had sex in three weeks. And, well, my laundry is piled to the ceiling and my house is a mess. My five-year-old daughter could also use a serious attitude adjustment. I really wish I had time to get a haircut. And I hate to admit it, but my son's first word was "Shrek."

Us: *OK, things aren't perfect. But overall, are you happy?*

Them: Umm, wow, *happy*? Well, yeah. I mean, yeah, I'm happy. Well, I wouldn't say *totally* happy. You know, I have an MBA. Why can't I do this? *[Long pause.]* I feel like such a bad mom sometimes. This isn't really what I expected.

Wondering why so many mothers are feeling overwhelmed, stressed, guilty, and stretched? Wonder no more. We judge ourselves, we compare ourselves to others we think have it all together, we feel out of control. We have more "bad mom" days than "good mom" days. We're struggling to find balance, and we've lost sight of our identity. One mom told us an all-too-familiar story. "I remember when Ellie was turning one, I wanted to make her cake. I had gotten the *Martha Stewart Baby* magazine, and it was all about making the first birthday cake special, being made by you. So I almost killed myself making this cake and decorating it, and screwed up the monogram on top! I was so stressed out that I started screaming at my husband and we got in a huge fight."

We also tend to feel alone in this particular brand of insanity because so few people are talking honestly about how they feel in motherhood today. We expect the world of ourselves, and we think everyone else is just bearing up under the burden better than we are. As another mom, Marissa, told us, "I'm dumbfounded on a daily basis as to how you're supposed to maintain your house and all that entails, maintain and raise your children, have a great marriage and relationship, keep yourself healthy and balanced, and be interesting and have great friendships. I'm totally flabbergasted. Women are doing this all around the world? I totally don't get it."

DIRTY LITTLE SECRET

I really wish I would've followed my grandmother's advice and married for money.

HE LOOKS AT ME CROSS-EYED AND THINKS I'M CRAZY

Of course, our motherhood pressures affect our husbands, and ultimately our marriages. This usually takes the form of our husbands assuming we're crazy. After all, when he married you, you probably didn't obsess over having the perfect skirt to wear to your son's third birthday party in your immensely important role as Mother of the Birthday Boy. You probably didn't have all of these insane "shoulds" swirling around in your head, making you completely exhausted and overextended, and liable to snap if anybody so much as suggests, last minute, that you invite the neighbors over for dinner. As Lisa so nicely put it, "[My husband's] aware that most women are nuts. He's seen firsthand some other mothers and other women, and scratches his head. When he comes home at night and I'm ranting like a loony person about the mom politics I've encountered during my day, he just looks at me cross-eyed and tells me I'm completely crazy."

"He'd come home to this screaming baby and crying wife every day. . . . The fact that he didn't tell me I was crazy—that was probably quite a challenge for him. I said, 'Do you think our parents would be mad if I gave this baby up for adoption?' and he said, 'Uh, *yeah* . . . they would.'"

AMANDA, married 9 years, 1 child, San Leandro, CA

I WISH I HAD "THAT GUY"

Some of this is timeless, and some is unique to our generation. We were raised to believe that we could and should do it all. That if we picked the right combinations of *coulds* and *shoulds*, our lives would work out perfectly. We'd have great husbands, great relationships, great kids, great careers.

The idea that we can (and should) succeed at anything if we just put our minds to it has contributed to the difficulty we have admitting hardship in our lives. We made our own choices, right? So we should be able to shape our outcomes. And if we don't succeed in creating perfect happiness in our lives, it's not that life is hard and perfect happiness is a fantasy—it's our fault!

The result is that a lot of women don't want to talk about reality, because reality looks like failure to them. Our marriages, our family lives, our careers are not turning out as we planned, because what we planned for was perfection, and what we got is merely good. We know this is sort of nuts, but we're having a hard time letting go of it anyway. As one mom named Julia put it, "I know no one has this perfect fairy-tale husband who *talks* to you about your feelings and pitches in all the time, but I wish I had 'THAT GUY.'"

So, what we're left with is feeling embarrassed and self-protective about our lives as we actually live them—and this only exacerbates the expectations problem! In a crazy feedback loop, we compare ourselves to the outward façades of other people's marriages, not their *real* marriages. Then we assume our own marriage is not stacking up. (Maybe our husbands *are* onto something when they look at us cross-eyed.) "I do feel pressure," says another mom named Jill. "I'm always comparing us to couples who don't have problems, especially friends who have these great Hollywood marriages."

Excuse us—great Hollywood marriages? This is a recipe for misery. Most of our marriages are, or at least can be, pretty good, if not better than that. But we don't all live on a soundstage in Hollywood, and we need to be smart about what and who we compare ourselves to.

DID I GET A LEMON?

Another compounding factor in today's marriages is that, for the first time in history, staying married is completely voluntary, and that causes us to question whether we're in a good marriage anymore. Divorce is so commonplace, and so many of us have divorced parents, that it's accepted that we can leave our marriages at any time. This leads to some not-so-pretty consumerist questions in lots of women's heads. How's my husband functioning? Should I upgrade? Is he living up to his performance guarantee? Did I get a lemon?

We know he's a human being, and we shouldn't think of him as less than he was when we married him, but when we have fights, instead of just feeling sad, we feel buyer's remorse. We yearn to try a different model. Exacerbating these feelings, there's little social encouragement to stick with the status quo. A "disposable" attitude permeates our lives, almost always to our detriment. It's one thing when the TV breaks and we throw it away instead of fixing it. But it's quite another when we bring that mind-set into our marriage. We've probably never met him, but let us assure you: Your guy is not a lemon. You cannot, and should not, bring him back (well, not most of the time). Commitment really counts when times are tough. One mom we know reminds herself when her husband starts driving her crazy by making sausage in the kitchen on a Sunday afternoon—which to her eyes and ears is pretty much the grossest-looking and

DIRTY LITTLE SECRET

I secretly listen to my husband put our son to bed on the baby monitor in our room. I love the way he sings sweet and silly songs to him.

-sounding thing imaginable—"OK, this is the part when you're really married." That "for worse" phrase is part of the marriage vows for a good reason. If you expect difficulties, and commit to working through them, your marriage will be stronger for it.

"His qualities are hiding behind the qualities I *wish* he had."

JULIA, married 5 years, 2 children, Newton, MA

HE WANTS ME TO BE THIS COOKIE-CUTTER MOM

One good way to start unpacking the expectations of your marriage is to start thinking about your role models—what examples you're trying to emulate or avoid, and what examples your husband is trying to emulate or avoid. As Meg Newcomer, a family therapist, explained to us, "When we look at our partner, we see three people— them, and our two parents." (Scary, huh?) "How did we learn to cope with pain and difficulty, how did our family deal with conflict, show love, allow space for feelings to be expressed or not. You come into marriage with a suitcase of clothes, and you're constantly trying to fit those clothes on your partner. And a lot of times they don't fit at all! Or it's a shirt from your mom!"

We heard from parents at both extremes—from "We tend to model our current and future lives on how badly our parents screwed up," to those who are struggling to figure out how their own parents managed as well as they did. "I can't entertain the way my mother did, I can't have that house, I can't have the marriage she did," another mom told us. "And I'm coming to terms with the fact that we are the way we are, and that's OK. It's a daily struggle."

"He's really pushed for a third kid, and I'm like, 'You're smoking crack!' We can't do that under this model!"

MANDY, married 6 years, 2 children, Cleveland, OH

"We don't have too many friends who come over anymore because the house has to be spotless. She wants to have everything just so. For her, I really give it the 'sphere' analogy. As long as the outside of the sphere is looking good, it doesn't matter what's happening on the inside. She doesn't want any faults to be seen."

RICK, married 10 years, 2 children, San Rafael, CA

"Shoes, man. She has tons and tons of shoes and boots. And I'm usually the one who's picking them up. Even as we speak! That's one thing I didn't expect—I'm the shoe picker-upper!"

MARK, married 8½ years, 2 children, Chapel Hill, NC

Whatever's the case for you—hellish parents or saintly ones—just thinking about your role models can go a long way.

- ○ Are you trying to be as good a mother as your mother?

- ○ Is your husband trying to be a better dad than his dad?

- ○ Do you know more about what you *don't* want your marriage to look like than what you *do* want your marriage to look like?

- ○ Are you feeling conflicted about the role you're playing in your marriage?

- ○ Are you feeling guilty for not being the husband or wife you think you should be?

A lot of women told us they feel like guinea pigs, trying to navigate a workable path through marriage in a world where women's roles have changed so quickly. Your husband's mother and your own mother probably carried very different roadmaps for getting through their lives. "He grew up in a traditional home; his mom did everything and he expected that for us," Sara told us. "Generationally, it's not like that anymore. We as wives expect more of our husbands now. We expect them to pitch in more! As far as any other issues— the parenting aspect—we didn't realize we'd come out on such different sides of the fence. He very much wanted a wife to stay home. He saw this cookie-cutter mom at home and wanted that from me."

HE'S THE FUN DAD AND I'M THE MEAN MOMMY

This lack of current models has led to a lot of confusion over the roles we're all supposed to play.

Some men and women told us they thought it would have been easier to be happily married (and to be co-parents) a generation ago, when gender roles were more strictly defined. Whether or not this is actually true is debatable. But it does seem to highlight the fact that roles within a marriage can be a big source of tension. Many of us come into marriage with unspoken views of what *his* role and *her* role are going to be. Sometimes our views are compatible with our spouse's, and sometimes they're not. And if they're not, that can lead to a whole lot of tears and tension. One mom, Georgia, told us, "I do get angry. We argue about what our roles are. I say, 'I'm not asking you to *help* me; I'm asking you to *parent* with me.'"

Other men and women thought it should be easier to be happily married *now*, in that many couples start off down the aisle as equal partners, and *equal* seems like a really good position from which to create a shared life. But this, too, has its set of perils. Many marriages that strive to be equal partnerships often wind up looking like see-saws, with a lot of shifting of who is up and who is down (and a lot of bruised backsides and egos when positions change). Worse, some marriages that strive for equality start to look like tugs-of-war, with each spouse pulling hard to retain equal standing in a house that's getting rocked by kids.

Believe us, we're all for equality. We just want to raise the idea that "equal" is a *goal*, not a fixed setting on a thermostat. And it is maddeningly difficult to attain. "Here's my take," says Barry Schwartz, author of *Paradox of Choice*. "There's been a lot of attention paid to the amount of work women do in the household. But it's not really equal. I think what hasn't been focused on is the emotional and mental work—namely, who makes the decisions. This is incredibly important: Even if the husband's around, and shares the kid workload, who's making the decisions about playdates, schools?

DIRTY LITTLE SECRET

My husband has no idea that I wax my eyebrows—he would be mortified—he has no idea that appearing so low maintenance is so high maintenance (and costly).

The overwhelming, crushing responsibility of it all still lies with the mother. It's a false sense of being equals."

The emotional valences of different parents doing different chores can also interfere with equality. "He's the 'fun dad.' It's the weekend—it's time for McDonald's, playing baseball in the drive-way—let's go out for bagels," one mom named Lisa told us. "I look bad, because I'm the mean mommy who has to feed them breakfast before school and not go out for bagels."

"I married a man who has *no* interest in *any* culinary arts—like none. Not boiling eggs, not boiling pasta—nothing. I didn't think about this, and I didn't think that it would be such a big deal. If I were to assign him a dinner once a week, it would be pizza. It's OK I guess, but I kind of don't want to eat pizza."

MARISSA, married 5 years, 2 children, Hanover, NH

MONEY MONEY MONEY

Money also impacts marriages in crazy ways, whether we want it to or not (and talking about this is one of the biggest taboos of all).

The stay-at-home moms we spoke to were surprised at how pow-erless they sometimes felt in their marriages, especially when it came to decisions around big-ticket items, like houses and private school. "We had this whole argument over schools—private versus public.

And I felt powerless," one full-time mom explained. "I felt like I couldn't make the decision. He didn't want to spend the money, and I thought my vote didn't count as much [being] a stay-at-home mom."

Families in which the mother was the main breadwinner also had their share of bumps. "There is nothing less sexy than your husband saying, *You're the breadwinner*," one mom admitted. "The pressure is on me. What about *my* choices? Why aren't *I* the mom?" Another mom shared, "I had this conversation with myself this morning driving in the car: 'Jennifer, you knew what you were getting into! You *knew* you would have to be the breadwinner! You *knew* that this would be the deal.'"

Another mom said, "It all sounded so wonderful: He would work, I would stay home. I remember my dad saying to me, 'Money is power. You need to take care of yourself.' In the next breath, he would say, 'You need to get married and be taken care of.'"

"What he wants is a part-time career woman who can add to the bottom line, and a great stay-at-home mom who can take care of everything domestic, everything at home, for us and our kids. You've got to be a black belt on both sides."

SHANA, married 4 years, 2 children, San Jose, CA

DIRTY LITTLE SECRET

I wish my husband traveled for work. I would love to have nobody talk to me at all. It would be a dream.

"I will try for 'forever,' but if it doesn't work, oh well."

JOAN, married 2 years [now separated], I child, Oakland, CA

"I had to reset my expectations for my marriage after kids. Yeah, we were arguing; yes, there was no sex . . . but I thought, 'OK, this is really hard. Remind yourself who you are, who he is, and what is good about *us*.' But I have to force myself to have that conversation with myself on a regular basis."

JESSIE, married 8 years, 2 children, Winston-Salem, NC

Men:

THEIR PERSPECTIVES, THEIR PRESSURES

. . .

Husbands and fathers today face a lot of pressures that we don't necessarily understand, or ask about, or give them credit for. We're so wrapped up in all that we need to do—our whole "perfect mom" trip—that we fail to appreciate that they, too, might be feeling overwhelmed. Like us, our guys feel obligated to do it all, and do it all well. As Meg Newcomer, a family therapist, explains, "Men feel unappreciated sometimes. They think, 'I'm providing, so why am I getting yelled at? I would rather be at soccer.' There's a lot of talk about Supermom, but what about Superdad?"

The truth is, the same stuff that keeps women off balance and anxious in motherhood has made fatherhood difficult for men. They have no roadmap to show them how to be a good husband and a good dad. They feel pressured to provide. They feel pressured to be "present." Men feel so many pressures from so many different places that many are caught off guard when their wives start insinuating that husbands today are getting the better deal. So if you haven't clued into this already, it's time you do: Many contemporary fathers are feeling lost, unsure of who they are and even who they're supposed to be. For our guys, too, gender roles are less clear-cut than they were a few decades ago. That leaves our husbands bumbling around, getting banged up by all the demands they put on themselves, and making up their roles as spouses and parents as they go along.

"The pressures as a father—to be there, be present, give the gift of time with my children . . . I feel extremely pressured that I don't have quality time with them. The other pressure is financial. You're always trying to gain the right finances to have the time. But as you get more and more entrenched in your career and climb the ladder, it takes you away. It's always a struggle to make enough money and have enough time! The biggest pressure is to make the time I spend with my wife and kids *quality* time. Sometimes that's hard to do."

NED, married 19 years, 2 children, San Francisco, CA

"We got pregnant immediately, and it turned out my husband was not as ready as he thought he was. A weird switch went off when I got pregnant—he was *not* into it—he didn't show any excitement at all. He was flatline. I was very sad and very anxious about it. But I tried to give him the space he needed, and finally he embraced it in his own way."

BETH, married 5 years, 1 child, Seattle, WA

"Most guys I know in committed relationships are giving up a lot, without getting credit for it."

BRIAN, married 10 years, 3 children, Orlando, FL

"I get resentful of the sacrifices I've had to make. Sometimes I get frustrated with the high standards about what we feed our kids, how we take care of them, what kinds of opportunities we give them. We eat a lot of home-cooked meals that are labor intensive, then we make a bedtime snack together and then have the bedtime ritual. We also give our kids every opportunity to nap; we don't push them into activities. But there are a lot of parties and events that we miss because we made this decision to raise our kids this way."

JOHN, married 7 years, 2 children, Amherst, MA

"As far as I can tell I'm following all the rules, but maybe things are being misinterpreted. I'm trying like hell not to step on the landmines right now. I'm walking on glass and I don't understand what I've stepped into. That little leeway—that little laughing things off—it isn't there anymore."

BILL, married 8 years, 2 children, Santa Barbara, CA

"PERFECT" IS A DIRTY WORD

So, what can you do to help align your expectation of marriage with reality?

The first thing to do is to remember that there is no such thing as a perfect marriage. Sorry, it's not going to happen. Same goes for perfect mother. You can drive yourself insane trying, but you're still going to blow it sometimes. Perfection is a fantasy, not a reality. So stop torturing yourself. You're a flawed human, like the rest of us. Welcome to the club.

It's also important to remember that all marriages, including yours, need to be reinvented after kids. "We had to do that dance to find the new 'normal' of that life with kids," is how one mom put it. We're not the same people we were after having kids, and our marriages are going to be different as well.

Lastly, you need to talk to your spouse about what you expect from each other and what each of you wants from your married lives. It sounds mundane, and a lot of it is—"I want us to go to the beach together," "Even if I'm sleeping I want you to kiss me goodnight." But think of it as spring cleaning for your marriage. Every once in a while you really need to air some stuff out. "It's something that we talk a lot about—how do you value your leisure time? How much weight do you put on keeping the bathroom clean? Sunday dinner? Taking the kids to church? Date night?" asks therapist Christine Ryan, M.A., L.P.C. "A lot of times couples are surprised at how different their answers are."

This, however, is not necessarily a problem. The point of marriage is not to become identical twins. "You're not going to share and love everything equally," Ryan continues. "I think what's important is to be able to identify what the other person values. Then you need to look at yourself and ask, What about me? What am I doing to enhance the marriage?"

"As a couple we are very strong. As co-parents we *suck*. In his mind, the perfect father is very successful at business and a provider—not making dinner. His mother says, 'A father can't be making international deals and sautéing broccoli.'"

MARISSA, married 5 years, 2 children, Hanover, NH

"My poor husband has cereal three nights a week. I feel awful about that—I know I should be doing more! I have this anger about having to do it. And I'm like, *you* cook dinner! I know that it's expected, so I rebel and don't do it, and then feel guilty for not doing it."

SARA, married 10 years, 2 children, Bucks County, PA

> "I hate that expression—'perfect marriage.' I don't even want those words to live in my head, like that word 'should'—it's a dirty, horrible word."

SHANA, married 4 years, 2 children, San Jose, CA

Just to be clear, we'll say it again: Contrary to popular belief, marriage is not about two people becoming one. You don't need to be mirror images of each other (and would you really want to be?). You just need to fit together. One mom we talked to told us she thinks the most important thing in marriage is to keep walking in the same direction. "I've finally made peace with the fact that our differences work really well together," another mom, Hannah, said. "He's probably more patient than I am, but I thought it would be the opposite. I'm more the perfectionist—wanting things to be a certain way. I'm more uptight. It's really great to have a partner to balance you out."

WHAT I WISH SHE KNEW . . .

○ "I wish she knew every time I tell her I love her, I mean it like it was the first time it was ever said. I never mail it in."

○ "I wish she knew how I try to help her with laundry and the kids, but I never seem to do it the right way. So I just shut down."

○ "I wish my wife knew that . . . football is only my 'second' favorite contact sport."

○ "I wish my wife knew that . . . the bedroom door really does lock. Really."

ways to keep
your expectations in check

1. Ask yourself what your expectations are for a good marriage. Do these expectations match those of your partner? Are your expectations realistic?

2. What expectations do you have of each other as a husband and a wife? Sit down with each other and talk about them (you may be surprised at how many expectations are imaginary).

3. Take a step back and assess where your expectations of each other come from. Did you watch your parents live together, happily married, for thirty years? Did you watch them live unhappily for thirty years? Did you watch them divorce? Most importantly, are the expectations created by your parents' example fair?

4. Consider how your expectations of yourself as a mother are impacting your relationship with your spouse.

5. Remind yourself why you got married to your spouse in the first place.

6. Stop thinking about what your marriage should look like. Redefine what a "good marriage" means to you, for this moment in life.

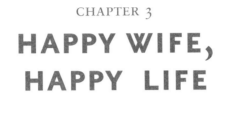

CHAPTER 3

HAPPY WIFE, HAPPY LIFE

• • •

(Make the Choice to Be Happy)

quiz *no. 3*

I know I would be happier if . . .
Check all that apply:

☐ The kids were just a little older.

☐ My husband helped more around the house.

☐ I didn't have to make lunches.

☐ There weren't so many field trips.

☐ My husband made me happy.

☐ My mother-in-law didn't make me feel guilty.

☐ There was no homework.

☐ I didn't like chocolate.

☐ I had more time to read/take a bath/do nothing.

☐ I lived near a beach.

☐ Dinner didn't come every night.

☐ My husband took the kids for a long weekend,
once a month.

- [ ] I didn't have to do laundry.

- [ ] We could take more vacations.

- [ ] I had a personal chef on call 24/7.

- [ ] My husband got a promotion.

- [ ] I got a promotion.

- [ ] We lived in a bigger house/I had a home office.

- [ ] I had a bigger car.

- [ ] We never argued.

- [ ] We had one more child.

- [ ] We had one less child.

- [ ] The grandparents lived closer by.

- [ ] The kids could run out the front door and play.

- [ ] We weren't too tired to talk to each other at night.

- [ ] I wasn't the one who was supposed to make everything better—spills, bruises, damaged egos.

We know, we know—

WE PROBABLY READ TOO MANY ROMANCE NOVELS AS TEEN-
AGERS AND HAVE DEFINITELY SEEN FAR TOO MANY MOVIES
with Hollywood endings, but we couldn't help thinking that marriage would make us happy. After all, we'd finished the hard part,
right? We'd met the right guy. We'd decided to spend our lives
together. We'd even managed to survive planning a wedding. So,
mission accomplished, right? We were married, we were happy, we
were planning on having beautiful kids, and we were all going to
stay wonderfully blissful for the rest of our lives.

This wishful emotional forecasting seems to reflect our assumption
that happiness and marriage go hand in hand. If you're married, you're
happy. If you're not married, you're not happy. But when we asked married women and men how happy they actually were, we didn't hear that
people were overjoyed. Women said they were "medium" happy. And
when we asked how they intended to become happier, they'd scratch
their heads and say, "Hmmmm . . . hadn't really thought about that."

The most surprising thing to us was how few women were doing
anything to make themselves happier. Part of the problem is that
most of us aren't completely unhappy. We're not in a crisis. We're OK.

Not good, not bad, just sort of so-so, and complacently accepting that that's where we're going to stay. But that needn't be the case. Your happiness, your emotional well-being, is largely up to you. If this book does only one thing, we hope it helps you to empower yourself to be happy—both for yourself as an independent person, and for yourself in marriage.

FOR MY MOM AND DAD, HAVING A HAPPY MARRIAGE WASN'T EVEN AN OBJECTIVE

Americans pack a lot into the idea of marriage. In our spouse we hope to find our best friend, our perfect lover, our ideal co-parent, our romantic hero, our partner in financial stability, and our fountain of happiness. But if you step back a moment and look at how people conceived of marriage in other times and places, you'll find that it wasn't until recently that happiness was considered part of the equation. People got married because it was expected of them, because you weren't supposed to have sex or kids without getting married, and because women needed to for economic reasons. And people stayed married for all those reasons, plus a few more. Because they were loyal. Because they felt they could not get divorced. And perhaps more importantly, because they said they would. Marriage was a solemn and binding contract. A commitment to happiness was not part of the vows.

"I think that for my mom and dad, having a happy marriage wasn't even an objective," one man we interviewed, Jim, told us about his own parents. "My dad fought in World War II. Feelings? I don't know if he even had them! He didn't expect happiness; he never saw it as the goal."

We're not out to suggest that happiness should not be your goal—just the opposite, in fact. But after talking with lots of married men and women, we did come to the realization that we need

"I think it's harder to be happy in today's generation. I remember as a kid, on Saturday morning I would go out to play, ride my bike, and come back for dinner. My parents would sit and read the paper, and enjoy their time together. Now we don't have that freedom. Someone needs something all the time, and kids have to be led around all the time with specific activities. Parents today just don't have the free time that our parents had. When I'm making dinner, my kids are right there. I bet my mother made dinner in a much more peaceful environment."

LUCY, married 10 years, 3 children, Greensboro, NC

"Now I know what life is like being happy. I thought I had everything on my 'list' with my first husband. But now I realize it's so important to know who *you* are."

SUSAN, married 10 years, 2 stepchildren, Walnut Creek, CA

to think about "happiness" much more carefully and proactively. We entered adult life with lots of big ideas about what would make us happy—a husband, kids, a job, a house. And while these are centrally important to our lives, they are not what we should be relying on to make ourselves happy. Complicating matters, when those things don't make us happy, we tend to blame our marriage, when in reality we can only be as happy in our marriages as we are in ourselves. The job of producing personal happiness is really up to us.

> "A happy marriage isn't my goal. I want a fulfilling relationship. If I had one word to describe Michelle, she's my partner."
>
> JIM, married 10 years, 4 children, Kentfield, CA

A PERFECT LIFE IS A LUDICROUS GOAL

There has been a lot of research about happiness lately, and one of the most important findings is that we tend not to be very good predictors of how happy or unhappy certain life changes will make us in the long run. We overestimate the happiness we'll feel when we get what we think we want. We assume the big new house or the promotion will make us happy—and it does, for a little while. Or we think that a loss will leave us permanently unhappy, and the reality is that we adapt much better than we ever imagined we could.

DIRTY LITTLE SECRET

My Brazilian waxer is the key to our happy marriage.

Another big happiness myth women keep bumping up against is the idea that because we have more choices and opportunities in a post-feminist world, we will be happier than our mothers were. Yet while women today can get advanced educations and have high-powered careers, the truth, as almost everybody knows, is that we are not whistling on a cloud. We are *stressed out*. We are *tired*. Sure, we're not feeling as penned in as our mothers were. But we are struggling—truly struggling—to find a way to be happy while trying to do it all.

Related to this is another misconception women seem to harbor today: that perfection and happiness are directly connected. We assume that if we can achieve absolute perfection in our lives, we will be absolutely happy. So therefore it must follow that if we can get our lives to be almost perfect, we will be almost happy, and if our lives are far from perfect, then we will be far from happy.

This seems kind of logical, until you realize what a setup it is. Trying to create a perfect life is a ludicrous goal. Instead of leading us closer to happiness, it leads us farther from it. We feel like failures as we continually fall short of our imagined goal—being that perfectly dressed woman with a perfect job raising perfect children with a perfect husband in a perfect, and perfectly clean, house.

"Humor used wisely and in a timely manner can get you through any situation."

GINNY, married 60 years, I child

"Having children brings you together in a magical way—you relive your youth together through their eyes. It's been powerful watching our daughter grow up, and it has strengthened our marriage."

ROSE, married 7 years, 3 children, Oakland, CA

"We each would say we've made a lot of sacrifices . . . I always rationalized the sacrifices I've made for my family, but now I see that a lot of those sacrifices weren't so beneficial. I thought more money and more success would lead to more happiness . . . I thought I could ease all the pain of life if I could take care of these issues. But our relationship has suffered from some of these choices. It's a shocking realization—those things don't take care of your relationship . . . *you* have to take care of it day by day."

NED, married 19 years, 2 children, San Francisco, CA

OUR LITTLE BUNDLES OF . . . JOY?

So let's talk: What the heck is going on? Most of us were happy to get pregnant. And happy to give birth. And most of us expected that having kids would make our happiness quotient spike. The problem is, we didn't realize that kids and happiness exist in a complicated relationship to one another. Yes, our children make us happy in many, many ways. But they also drive us nuts. They permanently change our marriages and our relationships with our spouses. Remember how much you loved how sporty and free-and-easy your windsurfer boyfriend was? Now that he's your husband and the father of your children, do you *still* think it's so cool that he likes to spend all Saturday offshore?

> **"The moment was here—I was finally a dad—and there was no real way to emotionally prepare myself for the reality. I wish I knew that things were going to be better than OK and that while the change was massive, it comes with a lot of pleasant surprises."**
>
> DAVE, married 6 years, 2 children, Corte Madera, CA

DIRTY LITTLE SECRET

I routinely hack into my husband's computer to see what porn sites he's been surfing.

Another thing we didn't quite realize would happen until we became parents was that we'd start to associate happiness with some future time, some imagined life phase when parenting would be easier. That we'd be happier when the kids were out of diapers, or when the kids were in school, or when they were old enough to be more self-sufficient, or when they packed up for college and left the house.

Literally hundreds of parenting issues tweak the happiness level in our homes. Hair washing. Doctor's appointments. Homework. Driving. Another major bummer (we might as well call it what it is) is the doling out of discipline and privileges. Do you agree with your spouse about when Johnny should get a timeout? Do you agree on whether or not he should have a TV in his room? If he's behaved well enough to get dessert? If his grades are high enough to sleep over at a friend's house? And it pretty much goes without saying: If you're fighting about the kids, marital happiness often goes out the window. It's hard not to blame a spouse—especially one you've been disagreeing with on parenting issues—when things go awry. *If you weren't such a softie . . . If you ever gave her a sense of freedom . . . If you'd just stick with her bedtime routine . . . If you didn't give in to his tantrums . . .* One mom we know calls these the "nevah evahs." These accusations are always tempting, but they're a recipe for disaster. Blame has made few people happy. Whatever the trouble, the key is to work through it together.

DIRTY LITTLE SECRET

Whenever my husband leaves the house, I secretly gather all of his old newspapers and receipts that he keeps piled up and run to the recycling center. Then I sit in bewilderment as he scurries around the house looking for them, thinking he's lost his mind.

WHY YOUR HUSBAND IS SMILING

How are our husbands doing, happiness-wise? Slightly better than we are. Today, men are ranked happier than women overall. According to a 2007 Wharton study, men spend less time on things that they report as "stressful," and they are less stressed-out as a result. We know from our own research that men don't put the same kind of pressure on themselves that we do to get it all done, and done perfectly. So putting their feet up once in a while and relaxing doesn't bring on the guilt pangs like it does for us.

After talking with many married men and women, we came up with a few theories to explain this. One is that women are still doing more than their fair share of domestic chores, even if they're also earning a substantial portion of the family income. As one mom, Sandy, said, "I come home from work, I'm tired, and it's still up to me to get dinner ready, oversee homework, and get the kitchen cleaned up. It's really hard to paint a smile on my face and lovingly say, 'Hi honey! How was *your* day?' when I'm in the midst of it all."

"I think men can compartmentalize more easily. She can't be happy with me if there's *one* aspect she's not happy about. I do think that's a difference between men and women. It's hard for her to overlook something and move on."

JOHN, married 7 years, 2 children, Amherst, MA

After 20+ Years

OF MARRIAGE, WHAT I KNOW IS . . .

• • •

"Kids leave; he stays."

> GRACE, married 25 years, 4 children

"The grass may look greener on the other side of the fence, but it requires just as much work, so be happy."

> LONNIE, married 55 years, 5 children

"After many years of marriage, what I know is that while staying in love is not work, you have to work at it."

> JERRY, married 45 years, 3 children

"Don't try to change one another, because it does not work. You really can't change a person without great damage."

> MIMI, married 58 years, 2 children

"He actually *is* right sometimes."

> GRACE, married 25 years, 4 children

"Respect the special uniqueness of yourself, your husband, and children."

> MIMI, married 58 years, 2 children

"It's what you do with who you've got, and never mind what he is not."

> LONNIE, married 55 years, 5 children

"After twenty years of marriage, what I know is that you need to cherish your relationship and not take it for granted, share laughter and a sense of humor, be willing to compromise, and say and feel "I love you" every day. Did I mention be willing to compromise?"

> VAL, married 45 years, 3 children

"I have learned after 57 years that I have to speak louder and slower—hearing goes in the male."

DOROTHY, married 57 years, 2 children

"Put your partner first."

CHRIS, married 23 years, 3 children

"After 20+ years of marriage, what I know is you cannot truly be happy unless you like who you are."

CATHY, married 37 years, 1 child

"Find someone funnier and smarter than you."

ED, married 50 years

"I decided to overlook the picky little things I didn't like and love him, warts and all."

GINNY, married 60 years, 1 child

"Only remember painful incidents enough to not repeat them. Once a lesson is learned, move on."

MIMI, married 58 years, 2 children

"Some sex is better than none."

JOHN, married 25 years, 1 child

"After 20 years of marriage, what I know is the best gift you can give your kids is for mommy and daddy to love each other."

CATHY, married 37 years, 1 child

"After many years of marriage, what I know is there has to be respect, friendship, communication, and above all else forgiveness. This all spells LOVE!"

KATHY, married 46 years, 3 children

"Discuss critical differences when fresh—never when tired or after drinks."

BILL, married 21 years, 3 kids

"Underpromise on all subjects and work like heck to overdeliver."

JOHN, married 25 years, 1 child

Another reason why men are happier than women is that women tend to have higher expectations for their happiness, and are therefore more likely to fail to reach those standards. (How insidious is that—being even more miserable because you've failed to reach your happiness goals?) Women are also more prone to link their happiness to things outside of themselves. *I'll be happy if my husband comes home and thanks me for making dinner. I'll be happy if my kids behave themselves well. I'll be happy if I can watch an entire episode of* Grey's Anatomy *without having to get up.* Then, if those things don't happen, we're not happy, when it might have been possible to be happy if we hadn't pinned our joy to external things.

WHAT DOESN'T LEAD TO DIVORCE MAKES YOU STRONGER

Another item crimping our happiness in married life is fear—fear of not being the same people we were before we had kids. Fear of not being as sexy as we used to be. Fear of not supporting the family the way we think we should. Fear of not raising perfect-enough kids. Fear of not earning enough money (for those of us who are breadwinners) or fear of being financially dependent (for those of us who've left the workplace). These fears are real, even if we wish they were not, and we need to face them openly if we want to get past them and be happy.

Some of these fears are as easy to allay as checking for monsters under the bed. (Take a good look. See anything there? Nope—let's move on.) Others, however, lie deep in our psyche, and we need to really examine them if we want to get past the problem.

One of the biggest fears we heard from married men and women was the fear of hitting some kind of marriage crisis, reaching that "dealbreaker" moment when married life as we've known it dissolves. But we were surprised to learn that an affair wasn't the number-one dealbreaker on most men's and women's minds. The number-one dealbreaker was losing the house or some other financial disaster. What's more, couples who had already lived through affairs were not so afraid that another would lead to the end of their marriages. They'd been through the worst and come out the other side. Some even reported feeling stronger for it.

"We came from a really simple start. I have our wedding picture up above our kitchen sink. It reminds me, every day, to reflect that we came from this. Even though some days are really tough, and maybe I don't have the perfect designer shoes, I can look up at our picture and see my bare feet, and realize that I knew that it was gonna work."

LUCIA, married 10 years, 3 children, San Rafael, CA

DIRTY LITTLE SECRET

My husband busted me Googling my ex-boyfriend.

In fact, one thing we heard again and again was that crises actually made marriages stronger. "I do think we got stronger because of hitting rock bottom—I made the conscious choice to make this a good marriage," one mom told us. Especially after years of sleep deprivation and diapers, it can take a good crisis to truly appreciate and understand each other as a couple again. Of course, it would be great if life were simpler and more straightforward and didn't require this, but it seems to be the nature of existence. *It took a crisis to make us decide to re-embrace our love* was a refrain we heard over and over.

FOUR BASIC INGREDIENTS FOR A HAPPY MARRIED LIFE

This doesn't mean you need to go out and manufacture a crisis. There are simpler ways to become happy. After talking with a lot of experts, we came up with a short list of the ingredients required for a happy married life.

The first is to realize that happiness isn't something somebody else provides for you; it's something you make for yourself. Happiness starts inside. An unhappy person with a great husband, great kids, a great house, and a great job is still an unhappy person.

The second ingredient is to realize that you and your husband may have different priorities, and that's OK. Willard Harley Jr., author of *His Needs, Her Needs*, asked husbands and wives to rank the importance of ten emotional needs: Admiration, Affection, Conversation, Domestic Support, Family Commitment, Financial Support, Honesty, Openness, Physical Attractiveness, Recreational Companionship, and Sexual Fulfillment. Guess what he found? "Nearly every time I asked couples to list their needs according to their priority, men listed them one way and women the opposite way.

"I spent all this time finding the right person, but have forgotten about *being* the right person."

SUZANNA, married 4 years, 2 children, Omaha, NE

"I'm happy that I'm a mom, but I don't like me right now. I think I'm gonna like myself more when I feel like I'm more in control of my life. When my kids aren't controlling me, and my job's not controlling me. I feel like I've been playing catch-up for so long. . . . It's like I'm being dragged along the back of a bus, just trying to keep up. Stop the fucking bus. Let's get a grip on this. This has not been working. I want to be in a healthier place so I can be more balanced for my kids."

NANCY, married 8 years, 3 children, Boise, ID

Of the ten basic emotional needs, the five listed as most important by men were usually the five least important for women, and vice versa." It's not intentional; it's just that we're coming from different places. We're trying to do things for our spouse that we know would make *us* happy. But our spouses might not appreciate the same things at all.

"Great long marriages are over in a flash."

ED, married 50 years

The third ingredient is to come up with a vision of marriage that is attainable and sustainable, and supports everyone involved. You've got to let go of some things, and readjust to others, without blaming your spouse. Aligning expectations with reality can be a challenge, particularly once we've had kids. But if we hang on too tightly to who we were before we had kids, resentment builds and happiness suffers. "I've learned to give up golf, but my wife isn't OK with giving up her stuff," one husband named Barry told us. But guess who's happier in the marriage? Being happy means making peace with your life, and not blaming your spouse for your losses. The harder you try to hold on to who you were before you had kids, the harder it is on the relationship. We talked to a lot of men who were really unhappy right after their first child was born. They felt like they'd lost their

DIRTY LITTLE SECRET

I keep a tally on a calendar of every time I have sex with my husband so if he throws a hissy fit about not getting enough, I've got a handy paper trail.

wife to the baby, and they blamed either her or the baby for it. Happiness only reappeared once they accepted their new reality.

Finally, the fourth ingredient of a good marriage is forgiveness. Not forgiving each other, for matters either large or small, creates ongoing tension. It's easy to say and hard to do, but forgive your spouse for whatever he's done, if you possibly can. Forgiveness will enable you to let go of negative feelings and live in the present. We all know what it feels like to live with resentment and anger, and those feelings can—and probably will—only worsen if forgiveness is not a regular practice in your marriage.

THE SEVEN-OUT-OF-TEN RULE

Central to creating realistic expectations is accepting yourself and your spouse as imperfect. One woman we interviewed, Trina, has decided to deal with this by coining the "seven out of ten rule." "I believe in the seven out of ten rule when it comes to your husband," she explained. "Everything used to bug me, but when I sat down and thought about it, I realized he has seven out of ten qualities I want out of a husband. Now I try to not let the three things he doesn't have bum me out."

Mental tricks like this can help you change the mood of your marriage, and fill your home with humor and positive energy instead of disappointment and frustration. The key is to take control of how you see things. Jack Canfield, author of *The Success Principles: How to Get from Where You Are to Where You Want to Be*, explains that you can't change an event—you can't change if your husband gets in a fender bender, or if your six-year-old develops a Bratz obsession—but you can change your response to that event, and that shifts the outcome.

"In the wintertime we talk on the chairlift, while the kids are off skiing. That's when we really talk. And ski together. A lot of our soul-searching happens on that chair. Are we both still committed to our careers? How do we feel about the direction of the family? It's so hard to enjoy each other's company normally. There are times on date night when all I want to do is eat the steak—I don't want to talk to her!!"

JIM, married 10 years, 4 children, Kentfield, CA

A corollary of the event + response = outcome equation is this: A happy spirit is contagious, and so is a grumpy spirit. We've all been there: You've had a hard day, he's had a hard day, and he comes in barking and yelling. You can't change that event—the barking and yelling—but you can change how you respond. You can yell "Fuck off!" and ruin your whole night in a huge screaming fight. Or you can say, "Wow, something must've happened today . . . what's wrong?" Guess which response is going to lead to the happier evening?

It's pretty simple, really: You can follow someone else's mood, or you can create a better one. Creating that better mood is work, but we all need to let go of the idea of happiness as a birthright and start seeing it as something we put energy into creating for ourselves and our families every day.

"What you sow in the early years you reap in the later ones, so keep your relationship a priority. It can be sweeter than ever or it can dry up."

GRACE, married 25 years, 4 children

GRATITUDE IS NOT YOUR GOOD CHINA

Part of creating a good mood is to look at the world with a "glass half-full" attitude, appreciating what you do have instead of focusing on what you don't. Feeling resentful? Let go of that feeling by paying attention to all the things you're grateful for. Research shows that expressing gratitude actually lessens depressive symptoms and increases the level of happiness. As Marci Shimoff, author of *Happy for No Reason*, writes, "People who are happy for no reason don't necessarily have more in their lives to be grateful for; they simply

DIRTY LITTLE SECRET

I never knew my husband was a nose-picker. It really bothers me . . . I can't believe I didn't know this for so long. And now he just picks away! He just doesn't care.

focus more often on gratitude throughout their day. The difference is where they choose to put their attention." She continues, "It's easy to take things for granted. How much time during the day do you actually focus on gratitude compared to the time you spend thinking about the problems in your life? We act as if gratitude and appreciation are our good china and our fancy tablecloth, and bring them out only on really special occasions."

Of course, we all face legitimate roadblocks to our happiness. We all have behaviors or even genes that have been passed down that we don't want in our lives and in our marriages. But if we can identify them, we can begin to work with them or around them, instead of letting them control our lives.

We don't mean to suggest that you should start running around like a cult-inductee with a fake smile plastered on your face. None of us is happy constantly, and emotions change much more quickly than some of us might think. As Dan Baker, author of *What Happy People Know*, says, "We know, for example, that women appear to vacillate from happiness to sadness far more quickly than men. When it comes to raising children, women say that it's both more difficult and more rewarding than they could have ever imagined. In fact, women experience more of all emotions except anger, and while they experience 2–4 times more depression than men, they also report more positive emotions more frequently and more intensely."

So how can we be happier? Researchers have found that we each have a "happiness set point," an emotional place we tend to return to unless we make a conscious effort to do something different in our lives. And that emotional set point is only *10 percent* determined by outside factors like money, marital status, and job. Only 10 percent! Some researchers have found that four out of five people post-divorce

To have a happy marriage
YOU HAVE TO BE HAPPY YOURSELF

• • •

Here are four steps you can take toward that goal:

1. Ask yourself, "Who am I today?" Don't put pressure on yourself to reclaim who you were before you got married and had kids. Start to figure out who you are *now*.

2. We are so busy trying to live up to others' expectations of what a "good mom" and "good wife" are that we're forgetting about ourselves. Do something for yourself; it will ultimately benefit the whole family.

3. Schedule time for yourself just like you would another appointment. Commit to that one hour—and make sure everyone in your family knows about it.

4. Reconnect with your goals, hopes, and dreams. Take one baby step toward them.

were still not satisfied or happy in their lives. (Of course, we didn't talk to all those people, but it's pretty safe to assume those divorcées thought their marriages were making them unhappy, when it turned out they were just unhappy, period, and their marriages could not fix that.) The key here is to know that, despite our individual set points, we need to be proactive about wanting to be happy and doing something about it.

As a mom named Shana said to us, "I could go to bed and be asleep when he gets home, or try to stay up and chat with him. To me, that's choosing happiness. It's not a mind-set. It's choosing to talk, choosing to be with him. It's unglamorous, but I know I need to stay up to say hello to him."

"After 20+ years of marriage, what I know is life is not always easy, and marriage is part of life, so know there will be bumps. Learn to talk to your spouse early on to discuss differences, to constructively resolve conflict, so that when the bumps do come you'll be better equipped to maneuver through them together."

CATHY, married 37 years, 1 child

HAPPINESS: USE IT OR LOSE IT

One last especially difficult thing about happiness—how do you choose between making yourself happy today and delaying gratification to build a happier future?

This is a really tough one, as delayed gratification is one of the hallmarks of maturity: If we all did only what would make us happy right this second, we'd all still be emotional teenagers with no jobs, no homes, and no degrees. But after talking to hundreds of men and women, it's safe to say that our generation has gone to the other extreme. We're all so worried about what it'll take to make us happy in the future—the beefy 401(k), the college savings account—that many of us are neglecting what we need to be happy right now. We think, 'OK, I'm pretty stressed-out at the moment, and I haven't relaxed since I went to the beach when I was pregnant with my first kid. But I'll be happy once my youngest child is in school, or I'll be happy once my husband gets his promotion, or I get mine." And then, of course, when that time comes, we may have forgotten how to be happy altogether.

One way to prevent this from happening to you is to think of happiness as a muscle. Like your quadriceps or your brain, your capacity for happiness needs to be used or it will start to deteriorate. Granted, it's important to think about tomorrow. It's important to imagine where you want to be in five or ten years. But so many of us are so worried about what we need to do to be happy in the future that we are failing to be happy at all. Which is a shame. To be happy in marriage, you need to be together when you are together. You need to focus on each other, right now, today. You need to create special moments with your spouse, rather than expecting them to just happen or going through the motions of "date night." We all have so much in our lives; we just need to enjoy the present.

And if working on happiness for yourself and your spouse is not enough, do it for your kids. If the adults in your house are freaking out, your children will pick up on that stress and things will snowball, leading to bad behavior and more strife. If you want to have harmony at home with your kids, you need to have harmony at home with your spouse (and harmony within yourself). "If you're happy in your marriage, then your kids tend to be happy," is how one mom, Maureen, put it. "The kids will start acting crazy if you're not nurturing your relationship."

"Marriage is hard. It's a lot of work. And it changes, every day. . . . I didn't realize it would be so fully connected to our kids' development—the diapers or the homework—how [that] would have so much to do with how our relationship shifts on a daily basis."

LISA, married 10 years, 2 children, Hingham, MA

DIRTY LITTLE SECRET

The same things I fell in love with him for are the same things that now drive me crazy!

WHAT I WISH SHE KNEW . . .

- "I wish she knew that the way to a man's heart is through his zipper."

- "I wish my wife knew that the kids do grow up someday and leave home!"

- "I wish my wife knew that telling her I had a good day at work is not meant to accentuate how bad her day was!"

- "I wish my wife knew that because testosterone runs through my veins, it makes me totally incapable of saying the right thing after she has had a bad day!"

- "I wish she knew how much I like taking care of her."

easy steps
to making the choice to be happy

1. Cut your partner some slack. Let him be who he is without judgment, and relinquish control of who you think he should be.

2. Pick three things that are essential to your relationship—e.g., laughter, respect, time alone, feeling cherished, physical touch—and make sure they happen regularly. Awareness precedes happiness. In order to create happiness, you have to be aware of what makes you happy, and then ask for it.

3. Spend a week eliminating things that make your spouse unhappy, and encourage him to do the same for you. For instance, turn off the phone or BlackBerry when you are home at night, or purposely go to bed at the same time.

4. Discipline yourself, for one day, to think about nothing but positive things about your spouse. It will help change your perspective.

5. Allow and encourage each other to get what you need—whether it's solitude or fun.

6. Think about one thing that's missing from *your* life and take a small step to satisfy it. (You never have alone time? Have a friend babysit for one hour per month so you can read a book or work out.)

7. Write down what worries you—what your fears are. Once you are aware of what's holding you back, you can begin to let more positive feelings in.

8. Keep a gratitude journal. Simply writing down what you're grateful for (even little things) will shift your mind-set toward the positive.

CHAPTER 4

SISTER,
he ain't your
GIRLFRIEND

(Communication Is Key)

quiz *no. 4*

Which of the following phrases do you wish would come out of your husband's mouth? *Check all that apply:*

☐ "Your haircut looks amazing—I love how your bangs frame your face."

☐ "I've decided to take care of dinner every night for the rest of our lives."

☐ "I just want to cuddle."

☐ "Come over here and tell me about your day. I promise I won't try to fix anything. . . . I'll just listen."

☐ "I can't believe you did four loads of laundry, made all the doctor appointments, did all the grocery shopping, made the beds, fed everybody a decent meal, got the kids to all their activities, *and* showered today—you're the best!"

- ☐ "I know exactly how you feel. . . . *Sex and the City* should've been on for one more season."

- ☐ "Sorry I'm in a bad mood. Maybe I just need more quality time with you and the kids."

- ☐ "*Both* kids have the throw-up flu? That sucks. You must be a wreck. Why don't you go finish your book and I'll take care of them for the rest of the day?"

- ☐ "How are you?"

- ☐ "Maybe we should make a list of my 'to do's' around here, since my memory isn't that great."

- ☐ "I think SportsCenter is a huge waste of brain cells, don't you?"

- ☐ "God, I *love* taking out the trash."

- ☐ "You've done enough picking up for today; let me tackle these dishes."

We used to sit leisurely,

SIPPING COFFEE, OR BEER, OR ICED TEA, OR GIN AND TONICS, CHATTING ABOUT ANYTHING AND EVERYTHING. ABOUT OUR jobs. About our parents. About our friends. About our wedding. About whatever was most pressing in our lives right then. We'd drink and talk, sometimes even ramble. And we did this with the blissful naiveté that we'd be having these easy, breezy intimate chats for the rest of our lives.

Then we had kids and—*boom!*—all that changed. We had no time to talk; sometimes no desire to talk, either. That guy that we did everything with turned into a stranger. The quality and quantity of our communication changed overnight. Gone were the girlfriend-style musings of our courtship and pre-kid days. In came the trench warfare–style patter of parents with too much to do, too little time to do it, and far too little sleep.

Talk became a necessity, a means of achieving a goal—not an expression of love. We've heard this from many couples: that contemporary marriages often start to feel transactional. After the kids come, the romantic part gets put on the back burner and replaced with the "Business of Marriage." "I feel like so much of our conversation now is about a series of little problems we have to solve: a playground scuffle or a classroom thing with our daughter," one dad said, speaking for a lot of us. "So little of our conversation is how we're *feeling*. It's [only] the nuts-and-bolts conversations." What do you need? Can you do it? Yes. No. Goodbye.

Some communication problems stem from lack of time, others from drifting apart. One mom said conversation with her husband left her "unfulfilled." She has a good marriage—she loves her husband, loves her kids—but intimate discussions in her house have gone the way of the impromptu weekend getaway. It's still a fantasy, but it isn't going to happen anytime soon, so she's decided to accept that and have her intimate conversations with her girlfriends instead. "I can meet a friend for a drink and show much more vulnerability with that friend than I can with him," she confided. This was a familiar refrain, one we heard from both men and women—those who'd been married two years and those who'd been married ten: *I'm having a hard time really communicating with my spouse. We talk, the basics get accomplished, but much remains unsaid.*

"It took two years before we even started talking about our relationship. Finally, we sat down on our anniversary, and he said, 'Oh, I've always been happy . . . so have you, right? And I said, '*No!* I've been unhappy for two years!'"

KELLY, married 9 years, 3 children, San Anselmo, CA

Why is it so hard to talk to our spouses? We're not going to recreate *Men Are from Mars* here, but we do share a basic working theory with the author, John Gray: Men and women are innately different—physically different, emotionally different—and that leads us to communicate in innately different ways. We'll get down to the details of how that communication is different in a moment. But for starters, let's air out what some of our communication expectations were when we entered into marriage.

When we asked women what they thought communication would be like with their husbands *before* they got married, this is what we heard:

- We expected our husbands to just understand our needs and emotions.

- We expected our husbands to be a bit more evolved—more interested in higher-order feelings, like empathy—than they actually are.

- We expected our husbands to reach out to us if there was a problem.

- We expected our husbands to be mind-readers.

- We expected our husbands to be our soul mates, to give us that magic, romantic, starry-eyed feeling, and be good sounding boards.

- We expected our husbands to be like our girlfriends.

This last point is particularly important and, though patently crazy, surprisingly common: We expected subconsciously talking to our husbands to be like talking to our girlfriends. And then we felt let down when our husbands didn't turn out to be our girlfriends after all.

All of us—yes, *all* of us—face communication issues in our marriages. We might think that the discourse is better between the Joneses across the street. We might imagine that our friends, cousins, or co-workers communicate more seamlessly with their spouses than we do with ours. But what we found when we talked to married men and women, coast to coast, is that communication issues run across the board. Of women interviewed for a 2007 Rutgers survey, 80 percent—four out of five—responded that having a husband who communicates his deepest feelings is *more important* than having a husband who makes a good living. Communication is the foundation of basic compatibility. It's the common denominator, the base. If you have good communication, you probably have a pretty good relationship. And if you have bad communication—sorry to say it, sister—if you don't find a way to make that communication better, you're pretty much sunk.

"I always thought I was working hard as a husband to do the things I thought I should do. I thought everything was great— I thought we had a better relationship than most. She never told me, 'Hey, I'm unhappy— this is not what I want.' I thought maybe she was just tired as a mom. I had no idea that she had resented me for that long."

NEIL, married 19 years, 2 children, Shreveport, LA

WONDERING WHY HE CAN PLAY A GAME OF BASKETBALL WITHOUT UTTERING ANYTHING MORE INTIMATE THAN "*SWISH!*"?

If you are like us, you probably have a few questions about communication and your guy. He's smart, right? So why does he spend so much of his verbal energy screaming at random motorists and/or the TV? Why does he insist on eating his breakfast in silence? Does he go deaf when the Sunday newspaper arrives? Why does he become suddenly and massively exhausted every time you bring up a relationship issue after eight o'clock at night?

We know how you feel. We've been wondering these things ourselves. But learning to accept that your husband is a different creature with different strengths and different sensibilities can help save your relationship. This can be a huge lightbulb moment in a marriage—when you finally accept that he's not a cretin, or even intentionally annoying. As one woman put it, "He's very understanding, he's very supportive . . . but he's still a man."

Recent research has shown that male and female brains start diverging from one another even before birth. In her book *The Female Brain*, Louann Brizendine, M.D., explains that after only eight weeks in utero, the female brain and the male brain (which until then are unisex) begin to go down different paths. "The fetal girl's brain cells sprout more connections in the communication centers and areas that process emotion," she writes. At the same time, male brains are growing more cells in the sex and aggression centers due to a huge testosterone surge. Adult female brains have 11 percent more neurons

DIRTY LITTLE SECRET

My marriage ended when he had an affair with a stripper.

"I just want him to be my girlfriend—to sit and chat with me—but he's not. And I'm getting mad at him for not being her. He says, 'Why are you on the phone 90 percent of the time when we're together?' And I say, 'Because you won't talk to me!'"

ARLENE, married 12 years, 2 children, Southfield, MI

"Marriage is a lot of work, but it's way easier than divorce."

KASEY, remarried 1 year, 3 children, Denver, CO

dedicated to language and hearing than adult male brains do. Male brains have 2.5 times more space allocated to sex drive than females.

Some of the brain terminology is esoteric, but if you want to get to know your guy, it's worth trying to understand. The prefrontal cortex, which is responsible for self-control, is larger and matures earlier in females than in males. (This may be one reason why women are more patient than men.) The hippocampus, which is responsible for emotional memory, is larger and more active in women. (This may be one reason why women tend to remember emotional events in greater detail.)

We aren't presenting these findings as a "Get Out of Jail Free" card for your husband. We're presenting them as a tool toward achieving a better understanding between the genders, and better communication. One simple way to think about male and female brain differences is to know that the male brain is set up to choose action first and talk second, while the female brain is wired the other way around. Wondering why a guy can play a game of basketball with his friends without uttering anything more intimate than *"Swish!"* and still leave feeling bonded and satisfied? Wonder no more. Studies have shown that women use about twice as many words as men. Women like to talk . . . and talk and talk. Men like to *do* stuff, and it turns out that men, in general, are happier than women, so who are we to judge?

I WOULD SAY WE HAVE A PRETTY "FAIR" DIVISION OF LABOR . . . I MEAN, SHE DOES MORE

There's doing, there's talking . . . and then there's understanding. One issue that was raised again and again was the amazing fact that husbands and wives can be talking to one other, even using the same words, and mean totally different things. Some words that have caused real confusion are *clean* and *soon*. But *equal* and *equal partnership* are also right at the top of the list. We say these words, and hear these words, and understand very different things. For a lot of women we spoke to, *equal* means "the same." Doing the same number of dishes, changing the same number of diapers, driving the same number of carpools to Saturday soccer games. But men seemed to define "equal" in much looser terms. *Equal* means "I do as much as I can and you do as much as you can." *Equal* means "I do more than my dad did when I was a kid." Even women in supposedly egalitarian, post-feminist marriages told us that while they strive for equality, they're not achieving anything close to a 50-50 sharing of domestic duties in their homes. Study after study has shown that women just end up doing more. Reasons for this abound: Women are better multitaskers; women have lower tolerance for dirty dishes, so they just do them first. Pick whatever reason you want; the reasons aren't important. Coming to terms with what "equal" means in your house is. One man gave us his definition more candidly than he intended. "Yeah, I would say we have a pretty 'fair' division of labor. I mean, she does more . . ."

So the marital 50-50 is more like 60-40. Or 70-30. Or worse. What's the upshot? It depends on your family, but keep in mind that the big risk of such an arrangement is not a bad case of dishpan hands, but a lethal overdose of resentment. According to a May 2007 *American Journal of Public Health* study, wives whose husbands were not very involved with housework were 60 percent more likely to be distressed, twice as likely to be unhappy, and three times more likely to be uncomfortable with their husbands. A similar study, by the Pew Research Center, found that "Sharing Household Chores" ranks

DIRTY LITTLE SECRET

I used sex with my husband to get new curtains. And then a new car.

third in importance for a successful marriage. Sixty-two percent believed that sharing household chores was very important to marital success. This is a growing issue for today's parents: Only 47 percent named sharing household chores as "very important" in 1990.

"My wife is constantly on me for not helping out enough. I was getting tired of being yelled at for not taking out the trash! I finally sat her down and listed the things I take care of—from paying the bills to planning vacations to taking care of the cars—and now we're getting better at appreciating what we both bring to the table."

CHARLIE, married 11 years, 3 children, Boulder, CO

One useful, and much overlooked, way to keep the resentment from growing is for you and your spouse to take the time to each detail how you're contributing, so that you both can make a more accurate appraisal of who's doing what. "Look at the facts," suggests family therapist and author Pat Covalt. "Scientifically break it down: 'You work X hours, I work X hours. You pay the bills, I do the dishes.' You *have* to be able to hear the other person, and hear their needs and perspective, and be willing to honor those. Men aren't always self-centered monsters. They often just don't realize what's going on."

"I don't think I ever expected 50-50, but I expected him to do a hell of a lot more than he does! He's improved, but yeah, *helloo*. He comes home, I'm wrestling kids, and all I can think of is him sipping scotch on his business trip! I think he should *want* to take over when he flies in the door, but he doesn't. It's far less than 50-50."

CLAIRE, married 13 years, 3 children, Dallas, TX

"I would've thought I'd be more adamant about housework being 50-50—but I don't think that now. A traditional marriage suggests some sort of profound inequality. That doesn't apply to us—it's not like I'm marginalized. I feel really appreciated—he always says what an incredible job I'm doing. The traditional model can be great."

LAUREL, married 13 years, 3 children, San Francisco, CA

This advice dovetails well with what we heard from a lot of women—that their men don't even seem to understand how much they're working. Nor, to be fair, did the men we spoke to feel that their wives understood their contributions very well, either.

"When I get irritated, I blame him. *Why isn't he being more helpful? Why doesn't he see that I'm struggling? Do you see that I'm a one-man show here? Get up off the couch and help!*" one mom declared.

Others just laughed at the concept of "equality," with one mom scoffing, "Division of labor. Yeah, right! I love him to death, but he's clueless. He doesn't even know what the teachers' names are. He doesn't know what's going on. He was trying to get my son dressed to go in the snow and put on this hot pink snowsuit, and he's screaming, 'It doesn't fit!' Do you think maybe that's not *his*? I didn't expect him to be *this* clueless. I thought he could load the dishwasher. He was trying to load the laundry, and asked me, 'Where does the soap go?' Some of it's me enabling him. How did he get to forty and not know where the soap goes in the laundry machine?"

I TRY TO BE NICER, SAY "PLEASE" AND "THANK YOU," AND PRETEND I DON'T KNOW HIM

It's one of the lousier aspects of human nature that we tend to stop appreciating what we already have. We think we'd like a new car, or a new house, or a new husband, when really the one we have is great, if we could only see it anymore.

Lack of appreciation—and its corollary, lack of respect—is a key problem in most marriages. If you don't have respect for your spouse, you won't have any desire to communicate with him or listen to what he's saying. Worse, he'll feel it, and naturally want to clam up. As a doorman in New York City wisely told us, "I've been married for thirty-five years, and the secret to our happiness is respect."

Part of the problem is that the act of expressing appreciation just seems to wend its way out of a relationship, like helium drains out of a balloon. Unless we make a conscious effort to keep appreciating each other, after a few years of marriage we'll drop below a critical appreciation threshold, both physically and verbally. Marriage counselors report a serious appreciation drought among married couples out there. "I remind people on a daily basis that what they promised to do is honor and cherish," says couples therapist Christine Ryan. "I'm not seeing a whole lot of honoring or cherishing going on." Reaching over and holding hands, or telling a partner he looks nice can really change the tone of a relationship. It's a pretty low bar, but Ryan reminds us, "If you're not treating someone like you would a co-worker or anyone else, there will be a problem here."

Part of the difficulty of marriage is that it's "forever," a setup that tends to make little things turn into big things on the theory that *I can't possibly live with his crumbs on the counter/the smell of his sneakers/heavy metal for the rest of my life.* Let's take a small grievance: Your guy is supposed to take out the garbage, and he did not. All too often, in the hothouse of a marriage, we take this oversight as a personal affront—*I can't believe he did that! He expects me to do everything!*—when in reality he just forgot, annoying as that may be.

Intention is important. Ask what your spouse's intention was before you assume anything. Therapist Christine Ryan suggests her clients take the time to parse out the issues in their marriages, and their intentions, in order to get to the bottom of a given offense. She groups marital problems into three distinct categories: Category 1 is "So what?" (So she doesn't cook the same mac and cheese as my mother.) Category 2 is "Can change and need to change." (We never make time for date night, but we need to.) Category 3 is "This is not negotiable." (We need to agree on big expenses for the house.) Categorizing things is helpful in keeping small matters from escalating.

One common communication problem for couples is that all fights quickly escalate to DEFCON 1. Keeping small problems small starts with keeping reactions small in ourselves.

There's no magic bullet for returning appreciation and respect to a flat-lined marriage, but many men and women we spoke to favored the trusty fake-it-'til-you-make-it approach. "I also just smile, smile, smile, even if I want to kill him," one mom on her second marriage told us. "I keep my thoughts to myself when I'm picking up his dirty underwear or changing the toilet paper spindle. (This seems to escape him, the advanced mechanics of this amazing invention.) He doesn't seem to know how to wipe down a countertop that he has just dirtied, so I just ignore it. I try to be more tolerant this time around. I ignore the little things."

Men seemed to be taking a similar tack, and—you know what?—when you're on the receiving end, it's not that bad. "I try to throw a lot of thank-yous out," said one husband. "I want this to *work*. I say 'thank you' because I'm hoping something will change."

"I try to be nicer, say 'please' and 'thank you,' and pretend I don't know him—that he's someone off the street. It's too easy to take that person for granted. If we're both aware that we're trying, then it's easier. If I feel like I'm the only one trying, then it tends to fizzle out. It kind of goes in waves."

SARA, married 10 years, 2 children, Bucks County, PA

"YOU'RE A GREAT PERSON IN THE HOUSE"—
THAT'S WHAT I'D LOVE HER TO SAY

So what do our husbands need to hear? In our research, one of the most common refrains we heard from husbands was that they wanted to be told how they were doing as dads (and they'd like to hear "great!"). So much of what we throw at them comes out as orders or complaints. *You need to be at the soccer match. You need to get them to eat.* Our default seems to be to criticize and demand, rather than to appreciate, and it hardly takes a great leap of cross-gender empathy to imagine how they feel about that! "You're a great father. You're a great person in the house—that's what I'd love her to say," a father named Mark told us. "I think I'd rather hear 'You're a great father' more than 'You're a great husband.' That accolade means more. I'd assume she thinks I'm a great husband."

"I do put pressure on him to step up and be more verbal and be appreciative—I need him to come home and say, 'Thanks for making dinner.' And if I don't get that, I won't meet his needs."

KELLY, married 9 years, 3 children, San Anselmo, CA

THE LOVE BANK

In addition to a steady stream of appreciation, another strategy that's effective in keeping the love and gratitude alive, especially when things get rough, is the idea of the love bank. The concept is pretty simple. Each spouse doles out an excess number of compliments, good feelings, hugs, kisses, praise, etc., and the ones that aren't required for day-to-day living end up in a virtual marital depository. Then, when that inevitable rainy day comes—when you're furious, and fighting, and sure that he's a jerk—you'll have a little respect and appreciation held in reserve, and that will vastly increase your chances of climbing out of a negative space.

Any means of communication is viable for filling up the love bank: face-to-face, over the phone, e-mail, even IM. A quick text message can really break the ice. As one mom told us, "I swear, e-mail has kept my marriage on track! We have busy schedules, and it's a nice way to stay in touch and connect. We talk on the phone, but when I get an unexpected e-mail from him saying 'I love you' or 'I miss you,' my heart skips a beat."

What's more, the mere act of *trying* to create a love bank will put your marriage in good stead. As John Gottman, Ph.D., author of *10 Lessons to Transform Your Marriage*, says, if couples have five positive interactions for every negative one, their chances of survival and happiness are fairly high.

THEY'RE NOT MIND READERS

That said, it's the male species we're talking about, and they may need a little coaxing to do the right thing. As we learned when we researched our first book, husbands today know they're not

DIRTY LITTLE SECRET

He acts like he doesn't live here sometimes. Where's the TV clicker, where's the scissors? Where can I find the packing tape? Should I put these clothes upstairs? It's YOUR house! Feel free to jump right in and participate. And you know what? I know where the scissors are, I just don't tell him.

supposed to behave like their fathers. They just don't know what that translates into in terms of action. We heard this a lot. Men don't want to be bossed around, but they do want to know precisely what is expected of and needed from them.

"The kids and I get into our rhythm, and he comes home and he doesn't know where he fits into our routine. I think it's easy to snap at each other—'NO! They don't eat green beans anymore, and she only wears her princess nightgown!' When I say, 'This is where we need you now . . .' it gets easier."

JULIA, married 5 years, 2 children, Newton, MA

It's not necessarily easy to come to grips with the fact that your husband might need detailed directions, but it is useful. One mother we talked to refers to her husband as being "on manual." He's functioning just fine; he just needs to be guided through all the moves. "I used to look to my husband to make me happy, and now I know it's a waste of time," another mom, Alisa, told us. "Unless you verbalize it, they're not mind readers. That's been a hard lesson to learn. I have these ideas in my head of what a man should do for a woman, and when he doesn't do it, I'm depressed! How does he not know to get me a ring for Christmas? Why am I getting a gift certificate to Sears?"

"Anyone who tells you their marriage is perfect and they don't fight is full of garbage."

GRETCHEN, married 4 years, 1 child, Lake Zurich, IL

"I worry about 'Am I being a good mom? Am I doing the right thing by still working?' No one gets 100 percent of me. Is anybody winning in this situation? I worry about the balance . . . trying to do anything well, and the impact it's having on my kids. Why is my five-year-old suddenly acting like a nightmare? Oh my gosh—does it have to do with me working? That is on my mind right now. Meanwhile, my husband worries about whether or not he'll get sex that night."

VERONICA, married 7 years, 2 children, Montclair, CA

WHY IS IT THAT
What He Says
AND WHAT WE HEAR
ARE SO DIFFERENT?

• • •

He says: Do you need me to pick up milk or anything else?

We hear: Is there no food in the house? Are you a totally incompetent mom?

He says: Wow, I can't believe Janet makes lasagna from scratch!

We hear: Let me think . . . when was the last time *you* made a meal from scratch? Oh, that's right—never! I can't believe my wife is so lame.

He says: Do you want a backrub?

We hear: I want to do you.

He says: Oh, you got a haircut?

We hear: Oh, you went to the ATM and lit a bunch of money on fire?

He says: Shouldn't Jimmy be able to read?

We hear: Don't you do flashcards with him? You're a bad mom.

He says: We should teach Lily how to ride a two-wheeler this weekend.

We hear: *You* should teach Lily to ride a two-wheeler. I can't believe you haven't taught her already. Slacker!

He says: You should go work out, hon.

We hear: You're fat.

He says: How was your day?

We hear: Did you spend *any* quality time with the kids?

IT'S LIKE I'M THE DOG TRAINER AND HE'S THE GOLDEN RETRIEVER

If spelling out what you want doesn't seem to work for your husband, don't give up. There are other tools to try. For instance, Amy Sutherland wrote a fascinating article for *The New York Times* about how she used animal training techniques on her husband to great effect. Her method was simple: Reward the positive, ignore the negative. And *presto!* Just like an aquarium-show dolphin, her guy began to do more of the things she wanted and less of what drove her around the bend.

"If we could just talk about it—that's what I wish for. He shows me he loves me, he feeds me, he does stuff around the house. I don't need him to *do* all this stuff. I just need him to be with me, use words, write a letter to me, just be tender to me."

KATE, married 14 years, 4 children, Portland, OR

Other women we chatted with offered variations on this technique. "I use kindness to get what I want," one mom, Annie, told us. "Sometimes men need to be patted on the back and acknowledged.

DIRTY LITTLE SECRET

I'm secretly putting off having him get a vasectomy because it allows me that one week when I'm ovulating to NOT have sex.

Sometimes I want to nag. But if I give him a little love instead, I know I can get what I want."

If positive reinforcement fails, you can always pull out the really big gun of communication theory: listening to him. Listening is something all of us think we do all the time, and something few of us do very well. "The biggest problem is that couples don't listen to each other," Pat Covalt, a therapist and author, told us. "Instead of saying 'I really want to hear your point of view,' most people have a need to get their thoughts across." According to Covalt, the first thing a person who wants to become a better listener needs to do is to become self-aware. "Ask yourself, 'Am I a good listener? Am I tuning in to what they are wanting or needing?' You have to be open, and willing to ask yourself: Do I have this skill? Am I hurting you? Do I need to learn how to listen? Recognize it in yourself . . . work on it."

"Right now there are piles of folded laundry that need to be taken upstairs, and he walks right by it every day. And it's like I'm the dog trainer and he's the golden retriever. 'Take it upstairs! Good job!'"

LILLY, married 12 years, 2 children, Scottsdale, AZ

By "listening" we don't just mean regurgitating what the other person has just said. We mean taking it in, trying to understand. A few women we talked to pinpointed a phenomenon with their husbands: Guys have a fix-it mentality. We tell them something's wrong, and they want to prove they were really listening by taking action, even if all we wanted was to be heard. Kendra told us she complained to her husband about the kids being overscheduled, and he immediately got to work on yanking them out of *all* of their activities. But this is not what she really wanted. She just wanted to vent.

"We never had communicated at all—to avoid conflict. Because I have a tendency to get angry and cry and take off in my car. Now we have a weekly scheduled communication, and no matter what we talk about, I'm not allowed to walk away."

JILL, married 6 years, 3 children, Pleasant Hill, CA

Other women complained of getting too little response. "One of my biggest pet peeves is when I'm trying to have a conversation with him. He has the ability to stay totally focused on SportsCenter while talking to me. And then he'll spit back exactly what I just said to prove he can still hear me," a mom named Margaret told us. "It shows a total lack of interest—but he can disprove that he's not listening in a second!"

PUT ON THE GLOVES

Finally, a word about fighting in marriage, because, as we all know, it's gonna happen. All couples do it, and that's fine—even good. You're not in a "bad marriage" if you fight. Fighting means you're still engaging with your problems. Silence means you've given up. In fact, a recent University of Michigan study found that married couples who hold in their anger die earlier than couples who outwardly argue. "The key is, when the conflict happens, how do you resolve it?" explains Professor Ernest Harburg, who led the study. "If you bury your anger, and you brood on it and you resent the other person or the attacker, and you don't try to resolve the problem, then you're in trouble."

Still, many experts have told us that we should all stick to a few basic ground rules when fighting with a spouse. For starters, don't be passive-aggressive. Don't entrench yourself in staying wounded—it makes problems worse. The best way to fight is to be straightforward. Just say what you need.

It's also important to shift your focus away from "winning" the argument and instead strive to find a solution for both of you as a team. Also, keep your fight isolated to the specific problem at hand. Don't start getting into larger, unrelated issues.

"He never remembers any fight we've ever had! He says, 'Why do you waste your brain space remembering them?' and I say, 'If you remember them, maybe you'd learn something!'"

MONICA, married 9 years, 2 children, Wilmette, IL

In addition, like proverbial Chicago voting, have your fights early and often. Bottling in negative feelings or hoping that silence will make your problems go away will only backfire and lead to more trouble, resentment, and explosions. Even saying something nice to prevent an argument is not necessarily a good long-term plan. "Sometimes I think that he spits out a compliment to get around having a two-hour conversation about something deeper," one woman told us. While it may avoid issues in the short term, that pattern is ultimately not constructive. "He wanted to keep me in this little bubble of happiness," another mom, Jill, admitted. "If there were problems or issues, he kept me in the dark—so that when he didn't have a choice but to tell me the truth, it was horrible."

Lastly, when fighting, avoid absolutes. Rule out phrases like "you always," and "you never . . ." These words put your spouse on the defensive and stuff him into a box. Don't blame, don't exaggerate, don't duck, don't shy away—just state your case, loudly if you have to. Whatever fight you're having right now in your marriage, you will most likely have again, and again, and again. Given that inevitability, it pays to learn to do it in a civil way. According to Dr. Gottman, 69 percent of marital conflicts never go away. Like your dog or your mother-in-law, your fight is yours for life.

"I just never take him for granted. And I really mean that. I try *so* hard not to end a conversation on the phone abruptly or badly. I never take for granted that these little things matter."

CHLOE, married 15 years, 3 children, Trenton, NJ

WHAT I WISH SHE KNEW . . .

○ "I wish my wife knew I understand that my worst day at work is better than her best day at home!"

○ "I wish she knew the real voyage of discovery consists not in seeking new landscapes, but in having new eyes."

○ "I wish my wife knew that I love her body even more now, since she has given birth to our child."

○ "My wife has no idea how brave I think she is. She delivered our first daughter via emergency C-section, and then we had some difficult first years of raising her."

○ "I wish she knew exactly the level of love and admiration I feel for her in those quiet moments, from simply staring at her across the dinner table, watching her make our son laugh, to simply holding her hand and walking down the street."

12

things you both can do
to connect and communicate

1. Take a step back and remember that you're one cohesive team. Even just using the words "we," "us," and "ours" will help reinforce that.

2. Sit down and tell each other specifically what you need. Resist the urge to make the conversation a competition of who did what, when.

3. Realize that most of the time, a person's anger or outburst is about them—not you. Learning that lesson will lead you to ask, "What's wrong, how can I help?" instead of taking it personally and getting defensive.

4. Practice appreciation—verbally or physically—on a regular basis.

5. Try saying thank you to your spouse for one small thing every day for one week.

6. Create a regular time to connect with each other, either weekly or daily. One mom we talked to has a 3 p.m. call with her husband every day to check in, even if it's just to see how each other's day is going.

7. Sit down with your spouse and ask him to tell you a few things you could do for one week that would make him happier—and vice versa. Is it giving him ten minutes of space when he gets home? Would his taking the kids out for ice cream once a week so you can read a book be a huge relief to you? Saying thank you for doing the laundry?

8. If you need to break the ice, send him an e-mail or an IM. Just writing "I love you" or "I appreciate you" or "I'm sorry" can go a long way.

9. Tune into the "invisible" things your spouse does for the family and let him know you're grateful. Does he take over with the kids at the end of the day? Maintain the car, gutters, insurance? Notice and let him know.

10. Look for patterns that have evolved in your communication—both positive and negative. It's easy to pinpoint what your partner's negative patterns are, but what are yours?

11. Remember that the same pressures you feel to be a great mom, he feels to be a great dad.

12. Don't have important conversations at midnight after three glasses of wine.

CHAPTER 5

WHO IS THIS GUY
and why is he
IN MY HOUSE?

(Prioritizing Your Relationship)

quiz *no. 5*

10 signs you need a date night with your man

Check all that apply:

☐ You celebrate your anniversary with a family trip to the zoo.

☐ The only wiener you've seen in awhile is Oscar Mayer's.

☐ You call him "Daddy" even when the two of you are alone.

☐ The most romantic thing you've said to your husband lately is, "I'd do anything if you and the kids could just let me relax for a few hours."

☐ You cuddle a little too closely with your Labrador.

☐ The last time anyone saw the two of you out alone together was in the hospital before giving birth to your last child.

☐ When you're trying to impress him, you slip on your "nice" sweats.

☐ His e-mail address comes to mind faster than his first name.

☐ You got a new job last month and haven't had time to tell him about it.

☐ Your most intimate moments with your husband occur in your dreams.

OK, so maybe you KNEW THAT MARRIAGE WAS GOING TO BE DIFFICULT. THAT IT WASN'T GOING TO BE AN ENDLESS STRING OF DATES. THAT YOU weren't going to feel that same breathless, romantic whirlwind until death did you part. But did you know it was going to be like *this?* Did you realize, once the kids came on the scene, that life had potential to become so unromantic so damn fast?

We're not just talking about your husband witnessing the all-too-animalistic tableau of you giving birth. We're talking about how you view your husband and your relationship to him. Depressing as it may be, nearly everyone we talked to told us about their slow slide from lovers into partners in "the business of marriage." We heard about lives overrun by practical concerns. We heard about "meaningful conversations" and—yes!—"sex" added along with "groceries," "work out," and "to-do" lists. We heard about spouses calling each other "buddy" or "roomie." And we heard—all too often—about how the "fun factor" had gone into semi-permanent hibernation. Some told us flatly they thought it had already withered and died.

Some women sounded naively hopeful, others cynical. "What keeps me going is I *know* we will get back there someday," one mom named Stephanie told us. "When our kids get through this stage, we will be madly in love again. I have to believe that. But right now everything's on hold."

We also heard from moms like Allison, who were all too aware that something might be permanently slipping away. "When we don't spend any time together, he calls us 'roommates'—'Oh hi, roomie!' There's no closeness, we're just robots in our routine. He's on the to-do list. If I can just give him a blow job for ten minutes, he's off my back for a whole day!"

Whoa—let's just pause here, sister. That is a dangerous way to live. If you want to have a loving relationship with your husband, if you want to enjoy your marriage, you need to nurture—and value—what you've got. And that means starting today.

SOMETIMES I LOOK OVER AT HIM AND THINK, "WHO THE HECK ARE YOU?"

Improving the situation with your spouse is not necessarily as difficult as you might think. We realize that relationships change and mellow over time, and that kids create enormous stress. But the single most common issue we heard from women about their spouses was not that something was inexplicably happening to their relationships. What we heard was that the *women were putting those relationships last.*

"I enjoy our little family, but he's like, 'What about me?' He feels like we've lost the 'we.'"

STEPHANIE, married 8 years, 2 children, Santa Barbara, CA

"I do put my marriage on a to-do list—we're on autopilot and I'm hoping my marriage is on track enough to survive this period of time, while my baby is so young."

ANNIE, married 3 years, 1 child, Boston, MA

"In my case, my wife turned into a kid, house, and *me* manager. And no one truly likes to be managed. I don't feel entirely respected anymore. It started with her leaving me notes when I got home—a 'honey do' list. It's a business relationship, and she's the manager."

RICK, married 10 years, 2 children, Sausalito, CA

Living
IN THE MOMENT

• • •

We've heard from many moms and dads that living in the moment is extremely difficult to do. But we've also heard that it's well worth the effort. The small moments of true connection we have with each other as a couple or all together as a family are what keep us going through even the toughest days. We can't have a date every night or a romantic getaway every weekend. But we *can* find five minutes in the car or ten minutes over breakfast when we're all there in the moment with each other. Living in the moment can go a long way in nurturing and building a marriage with kids. It's really easy to lose sight of "right now" if we're always planning for the future and not focusing on the little moments when we are together.

Life as we know it can change in an instant. Remembering how precious our lives together are right NOW can shift our attitudes, our energy, and our happiness.

Kelly summed up the general mind-set when she said, "The whole 'couple unit' is not the couple unit anymore—it's the 'family unit.'" Or as another mom, Charlotte, explained, "It's 99.9 percent about the kids right now. Even when we do go out, on our anniversary, we talk about the kids! I miss my husband. Sometimes I look over at him and think, 'Who the heck are you?' I wonder if we really know each other anymore. If we don't talk about the kids, we don't know what to talk about."

So how did this happen to so many of us? How did we come to backburner the couple unit to the family unit? The answer is pretty simple: We prioritized being good mothers over being good wives. Why? Because we felt tremendously guilty if we didn't always put our kids first.

We heard this repeatedly from moms coast to coast: The fear of being a bad mom colors a lot of decisions. What should you do with your weekday time? What should you do with your weekend time? What should you do with every waking minute (and a lot of the minutes you'd like to be sleeping, too!)?

Prioritizing children is important, sure. But children aren't the only thing in life. (Read that sentence again if you must: *Kids are not the only thing in life.*) Many of us have gotten to the point where we feel like bad moms if we don't put our children front and center, always. We're all for you figuring out what's right for you in your life, but we do think the idea that the kids *always* must come first is just flat-out wrong.

DIRTY LITTLE SECRET

I have a secret bank account. I use it when I want to make a big purchase . . . just for me.

Think about it this way: The backbone of a family is a good, healthy relationship between the parents. So one of the most important things you can do for your sanity, and the happiness of your household, is to sort out the conflict you feel between being a good mother and being a good wife. We all want to—and need to—be both. So you need to let yourself focus on being a good spouse. And you need to accept that being a good wife and being a good mother needn't be at odds.

"I feel a lot of guilt, and that makes me stressed—it makes us shorter with each other. We're missing out on an opportunity to have a great relationship."

KAREN, married 5 years, 1 child, Salt Lake City, UT

I WISH I WOULD HAVE KNOWN HOW TO KEEP OUR LOVE AFFAIR A SEPARATE SEGMENT

When we asked women about the conflict they felt between being a good mother and being a good wife, we heard again and again that the pressures of modern motherhood automatically put the children first. That the rules of modern motherhood don't allow for prioritizing adult relationships over the kids.

What? You're taking a vacation without the kids? We've all said this, or heard this—the implication being that taking an "adults-only" vacation is totally heretical behavior, like getting a tattoo of your ex-boyfriend on your back. Of course, everyone is jealous that you can take a vacation without the kids, and they also think you're very brave. But at the same time they let you know—in no uncertain terms—that you're not playing by the "good mother" rules.

Which brings us to the big question: Should you play by the "good mom" rules? And if you catch flak for breaking them, should you care?

Our answer to this is a resounding *NO*. As we heard from a few different therapists, the more kid-centric the family is, the more challenges the couple faces. A strong family needs a strong relationship between the two adults at its center. So while you may think that putting the kids first all the time is what's right for your family, if you really do that, your whole family will suffer. Not just you, not just your spouse. Your kids will suffer, too.

"One of the best things that you can do for your children is raise them with the role model of a happy, successful marriage," Wendy Jaffe writes in the *Divorce Lawyers Guide*. "Being a good parent and being a good spouse are not mutually exclusive." In fact, being a good spouse is a critical part of being a good parent. Your children learn how to have good (or bad) relationships by watching you.

What's more, if your whole family life becomes about your performance as a mother, your husband, naturally, is going to feel left out. "I think that sometimes he feels jealous or neglected because he isn't my primary focus," a mom named Serena admitted. "He sees me go the extra mile for the girls. I think that he doesn't understand why I'm not as carefree anymore."

"I went into this thinking it's forever ... but somewhere along the way I forgot you have to take care of the marriage."

NANCY, married 12 years, 2 children, Keego Harbor, MI

The men we interviewed seconded this: They felt abandoned by their kid-obsessed wives. In fact, they felt their entire family had suffered over the years from a blind focus on the children. "My relationship with my wife, that's last on our priority list," one husband, Ned, told us. "Our kids have always been first. . . . It was a conscious choice we made: to put our kids first, to put academics first. Now I wish I could change that. I wish I would have known how to keep our love affair as a separate segment and make sure that we made time for each other."

"Those qualities I fell in love with in my husband can get hidden if I'm wrapped up in just my daughter. I need to do a better job at being present with him, and he with me."

MELANIE, married 4 years, 1 child, Seattle, WA

ME AND THE DOG ARE IN THE MANFORT TOGETHER BECAUSE WE'RE THE LAST PRIORITY IN THE HOUSE

So, ladies, it's time for you and your husband to start paying more attention to each other. And in case you're really rusty on how to do this, we'll go over some basics.

For starters, make a conscious effort to appreciate each other on a daily basis. This doesn't need to be a huge deal. You can just let him know he's a priority by saying something unexpectedly nice to him, or sending him an e-mail in the middle of the day, or giving him an extra-affectionate hug on his way out the door. (And if he looks hot, by all means, tell him!) "We try to remember that we're not just roommates," Adriana explains. "We need to do little things for each other on a daily basis. I try to put a note in his suitcase when he's going out of town, or really listen to his problems and concerns. We try not to become complacent; we try to take the time and effort. That way we don't pick on each other or put each other down or snipe at each other."

If you've been saving up your appreciation for date nights, we bet your dates haven't been much fun. It's hard to jumpstart a flat-lined relationship in two or three hours. People have a way of retreating if they're not being taken care of emotionally. Take Brent, a husband and father who felt he'd been at the end of a long to-do list for a bit too long. "Me and the dog are in the manfort together. I paid $2,300 for a shed in my backyard because we're the last priority in the house."

"The order of priority is: kids, house, her, dog, and I'm somewhere pulling up the rear. It's not a fun place to be now. I used to be *first*!"

STEVEN, married 7 years, 2 children, Reno, NV

It's also important to remember to live in the moment with your spouse, to try to appreciate each other and connect in the time you've got. "All it takes is effort to still have that twinkle. And we lost sight of that," admits one husband, Peter. So forget about the dishes that weren't washed or the homework that wasn't supervised. Just be present in the time you have with each other. Seize those moments and protect them, whenever they occur. "Someone told me, 'Put your kids to bed early—it's the best thing you can do for your marriage,'" says Melissa. "We're always guaranteed from 7:30 on we're alone.

We call those times our 'fireside chats'—we have herbal tea and catch up. That preserves our couple time in our own house—we don't have to run away from our home."

Of course, running away together is good, too—and it's important to try to do this when you're still happy with each other. Don't wait for resentments to harden into animosity before you ditch the kids and go get a drink. According to Dr. Gottman, 80 percent of marriages break up due to loss of closeness. So make sure you tend your marriage. Don't just assume your love will come roaring back as a matter of course. "We're making a conscious effort to enjoy ourselves—not just happily coexisting, but [trying] to get back to where we were. To enjoy not just life, but life together," one mom, Tracey, explained. You and your husband have made a commitment to stay together, for better or worse. You might as well strive to make sure the bulk of your time is "better."

"Couples that come in and say, 'These kids are coming into *our* lives, we're not coming into theirs,' end up much better off in the long run," seconds therapist Christine Ryan. "Some of us start out understanding this. Others have to learn it the hard way." But however you started out, it's not too late to make amends. "We both had affairs, in part because we weren't making time for each other," one woman we interviewed confessed. "Kids were number one before. And now as a couple we're number one. The kids are soaking up everything they see—and if we have a beautiful, loving relationship, then that's everything."

DIRTY LITTLE SECRET

My husband went out of town and I had the whole house painted so he wouldn't get mad about how much money it was. And he never noticed.

"I kept reminding myself—I was not put on this earth to tell him how to live his life, how to be, or what to be. We are all individuals. If this marriage is going to work we need to let each other be who we're supposed to be. And luckily, it's working."

MEREDITH, married 13 years, 2 children, Ross, CA

"Every year, my husband and I write down our personal and professional goals, and we put it as a priority to spend alone time with each other. That turns into a date night every Saturday, no matter what."

TORY, married 9 years, 3 children, South Bend, IN

Reinventing
DATE NIGHT

• • •

Date nights—we all crave them. So how can you make the most of the ones you manage to eke out?

A couple of rules of engagement:

1. Don't monopolize the conversation with kid talk.

2. Alleviate any expectations of a perfect romantic evening.

It's also important to enable each other to let go of the stress of your daily lives. One couple we interviewed forbids any talking in the first fifteen minutes of their date. They each get to decompress and build some fun tension. Do whatever's right for you; remember where each of you is coming from.

Then there's the question of the date itself. There's no one right choice, as Tara Parker-Pope pointed out in a *New York Times* article called "Reinventing Date Night for Long-Married Couples." "The goal is to find ways to keep injecting novelty into the relationship. The activity can be as simple as trying a new restaurant or something a little more unusual or thrilling, like taking an art class or going to an amusement park. But several experiments show that novelty—simply doing new things together as a couple—may bring the butterflies back, recreating the chemical surges of early courtship."

If you're having trouble giving yourself a pass on another Saturday night of *Princess Diaries* and mac and cheese with the kids, consider this: Your children are watching how you conduct your relationship. They're going to model their love lives on what they've seen at home. Your ability to nurture love will be reflected in their future romantic partners, maybe even their future self-esteem. It will definitely affect what they consider to be acceptable in terms of what a future partner gives to them. If you've got a kid who's asking, "How come you never kiss Daddy?" it might be wise to reassess what kind of love relationship you're modeling. Part of being a parent is showing your kids what it means to be a healthy adult. You don't want your sons and daughters calling their future spouses "roomie," do you?

> ## "If you put your marriage last, all 'systems' break down. It's hard to get it back."
>
> GREG, married 9 years, now separated, 1 child, Mill Valley, CA

YOU CAN'T HAVE A STRONG MARRIAGE WITHOUT TAKING CARE OF YOURSELF

Chances are, your husband is not the only adult in your household being neglected these days. You probably are as well.

In the quest to create a "happy family unit," we tend to lose sight of what we need ourselves. This can be OK in small doses—your toddler's need to eat breakfast trumps your own desire to read the newspaper. But if you *never* come first, it's going to catch up with you. Just like you can't have a strong family without a strong marriage, you can't have a strong marriage without taking care of yourself.

In case you're dubious, consider this: In our interviews we asked moms to prioritize, in order of importance, themselves, their spouses, their children, their homes, their jobs, etc. And more times than not, they would completely forget to list themselves! They were not a priority *at all*!

Counterintuitive as it may seem, we owe it not just to ourselves but to our families to define and then commit to meeting our personal needs. Do you need exercise? Do you need quiet? Do you need

DIRTY LITTLE SECRET

My husband was so NOT into the baby, but I never told anyone.

to earn some money or learn to paint? Figure out what it is you need. Then tell your family you're going to do it. (And then do it!) If you must, think about it as serving them in some way. What you do for your family is vitally important. And just as a mountain rescuer who gets hurt himself is no help at all, you're not going to do your family any good if you don't find a way to remain strong.

We also owe it to our spouses, strange as that might seem. They were drawn to us, in particular, for the qualities that we had before we had kids. We need to unearth those qualities and nurture them again as part of staying healthy and keeping life at home interesting and fun. This may take some tweaking to fit into your new life. (We realize that time is the scarcest currency in families with kids.) But even women who had extreme lifestyles before they had children manage to find a way. "I used to run marathons and climb mountains, so I've had to learn different ways to take time out for myself," an athlete mom, Stella, told us. "I can't do three-hour bike rides on Saturday. Life's a series of tradeoffs. You have to be willing to prioritize. You have finite amounts of time. You figure out what's important."

"There is a connection between us, but it's like this really tight elastic that could snap at any minute . . . but we're still hanging in there. It's frayed, but it's still there."

VERONICA, married 7 years, 2 children, Montclair, CA

TAKE A LESSON FROM YOUR HUSBAND: LOSE THE GUILT

Another important step to take in terms of priorities is to stop always defining yourself relative to other people—as a "good mom" or "good wife." Who are you, *alone*? What's the best version of yourself? How can you be that person right now in your life? In order to be happy and stay happy, you have to stay true to who you are. The point of marriage is not to merge into a single codependent being. The point of marriage is to love and sustain each other and your kids.

"Sometimes I don't have the energy to be a good mom *and* a good wife. Everyone ends up suffering. It never ends up feeling like enough for anyone, including myself."

LARA, married 3 years, 2 children, Houston, TX

Frankly, a lot of us could learn a little from our husbands, who don't feel bad about taking time for themselves. How come men don't have to ask for permission to go out for drinks after work? How can they jump on their bikes for a three-hour ride on a Saturday without feeling guilty? Part of the answer is that we let them, but another part is that they know they need these things, and they make sure we get the picture. (And, oh yeah—they don't have the "guilt gene.") Says one mother, Jemma, "If I give him lots of alone time or let him work out—if he feels like he's got a reserve of time for 'him'—then I know we'll be better off as a couple, too."

The same goes for you: If you love somebody, you need to enable that person to be who they need to be. Sure, you need time to be with your kids. You need time to be with your spouse. But you also need time to be with *yourself*, pursuing what's most important to you. If your husband doesn't get this, sit down and explain it to him. (Same goes for your kids, if they're old enough to understand.)

"To be a good mom and wife I have to do something for myself," is how one mom, Katrina, put it. Being a wife and a mother is not a temporary situation. If we want to be married for a long time, we need to make decisions that are sustainable in the long run.

WHAT I WISH SHE KNEW . . .

○ "I wish she knew that we're broke."

○ "I wish my wife knew that I may surf porn, but I'm indebted to her, for life."

○ "I wish she knew she's beautiful inside and out, and time only makes me fall deeper in love with her."

○ "I wish she knew her love for photography and passion for life keeps my interest in her growing and growing."

DIRTY LITTLE SECRET

I call my husband's friends and secretly arrange for a "guys weekend" but make it seem like "his" idea. I pick a huge "fight" with him about it, how lucky he is, and he has no idea that I like it. He thinks he "owes me one." He says, "Maybe you should go have a spa day with a friend honey!" And I laugh. It's sneaky but it works.

ways to put your marriage
—and you—higher on the priority list

1. Make time to reconnect, either planning a date night or setting aside an hour every night after the kids go to bed.

2. Same goes for you—carve out time every week to nurture yourself. Remember that if you don't take care of yourself, you won't be any good to anyone else.

3. Spend some conscious time every day thinking about what your spouse *does* do positively—even if it's just appreciating him taking the kids to school, or unloading the dishwasher.

4. Keep in mind that you can create your own special time together without leaving the house. Put the kids to bed a little early once a week, or send them to their rooms to play while you cook dinner together. Even just making intimate eye contact across a crowded (or kid-filled) room can go a long way toward nurturing your life together.

5. Think about your life goals and take steps toward achieving them. Your family will love you for it—even if they have to adjust.

6. When you are together, be together. If you're out of practice, this might take work. Make sure you don't let distractions and resentment get in the way of your couple time.

7. Write down what makes you happy together—and commit to making that happen more often.

CHAPTER 6

IF I HAVE SEX FOR ONE MONTH STRAIGHT,

will it buy me the

WHOLE YEAR?

(Make Sex a True Investment
in Your Marriage)

quiz *no. 6*

Have you ever ranked the following
above having sex?

Check all that apply:

☐ Clipping your toenails

☐ Clipping your child's toenails

☐ Showering

☐ Paying bills online

☐ Reading *Harry Potter* to the kids—again

☐ Reading *People* magazine

☐ Folding the laundry

☐ Thinking about folding the laundry

☐ Reorganizing the bathroom drawers

☐ Yardwork

☐ Sleep

☐ Calling your in-laws

☐ Wrapping birthday presents

☐ Scrapbooking

☐ Painting sample color swatches on the garage doors

So we've finally arrived

AT THE CRUX OF THE MATTER: SEX. IF YOU'RE LIKE ALMOST
EVERYBODY WE INTERVIEWED, YOUR SEX LIFE PROBABLY TOOK
a pretty good hit between the time you conceived your first child and
that child was born. A cruel irony, really: children are the natural
consequence of a healthy sex life, and as soon as you pop one out—
or even pop one in—that healthy sex life is kaput. You're exhausted,
misshapen, irritable, out of step with your husband, and desperate
only for a fluffy pillow, crisp cotton sheets, and eight hours of uninter-
rupted peace. But committing yourself to sleep—and sleep only—
is no answer to your problems. Because while it might seem like cutting out sex for a while is a great idea—what better way to jettison
some physical and emotional responsibility and simplify your life!—
pretty soon your husband is going to start griping, you're going to
lose some connection with each other, and your whole family will
start to feel like it's falling apart.

Sex and marriage are inalienably attached to one another, though
not always prettily or peacefully. At times the two seem meant to be
together (like, say, on your honeymoon), and at others the combi-
nation is a monstrous disaster (like, say, when you've just returned

from a round of vaccinations at the pediatrician and your husband has just returned from a business trip). Marriage itself is probably more to blame than sex for this. When we asked men and women if they thought marriage was a natural state, the answer was over-whelmingly *no*. Marriage is long, hard, and bears little resemblance to our fantasies of it. As one mom told us, "I've learned to think of marriage as being like meditation: You do it for a long time, and a lot of that time you feel like you're struggling, but the whole point is to keep striving in hopes that at some point you achieve a few moments of bliss."

Of course, achieving that bliss is partly dependent on aligning one's expectations of marital sex with reality—no simple trick! We're constantly bombarded with fantasy versions of sex. We see sexual images in movies, videos, and magazines, yet we have almost no reality outside our own experience to compare those pictures against. The result is that what we see in the media starts to seem normal, and what we live out in our bedrooms begins to seem pathetic and lacking.

Compounding the problem, friends and family often do very little to dispel the illusion that there is a lot of great sex going on in their homes. This happens either because (a) we don't talk to them about sex at all, or (b) if we do we discuss it, those conversations are edited down to just the juicy bits, leaving all the misfires, snubs, and aborted attempts undiscussed on the cutting room floor. It's not necessarily purposeful; many times we're just trying to live up to the popular illusion.

DIRTY LITTLE SECRET

I COULD come home for dinner, but I work late instead. Why come home to two screaming kids and a bowl of cereal?

Even in researching this book, we had our fair share of days when we felt lame and inadequate. One mom from Long Island, Sheila, told us all about how she's the queen of blow jobs and her libido is in overdrive. We wondered, *What's wrong with us?* Of course, after we took the time to ask her some more questions, about thirty minutes later we finally got to the truth that Sheila's sex life was a little less puffed up than it first sounded. (Turns out they had hot, steamy sex on their anniversary a month ago, but haven't had it since.) If the only sex we ever see or hear about outside our own is glorified or exaggerated, we quickly get down on ourselves. We feel we're not having enough sex. We feel we're not having sexy enough sex. Throw in the fact that sexual passion in all relationships cools over time—we're probably not having as much sex or as exciting sex as we used to have—and we begin to feel truly defeated and lame.

"Marriage is a natural state to get into; it's an unnatural state to stay in."

RANDY, married 7 years, 3 children, Mill Valley, CA

I FINALLY FIGURED OUT HOW MANY TIMES A WEEK WE NEED TO HAVE SEX

We all go into marriage thinking that a good marriage is full of good sex. But does that mean a marriage that isn't full of good sex is necessarily bad? And just how much sex, exactly, is required to keep a marriage *good*? And when did sex go from being one of the most fun things in the relationship to a compromise and a burden, anyway?

These are questions that plague lots of parents, and they don't have easy answers like, "no," "twice a week," and "six months into your first pregnancy" (though those answers pop up with considerable frequency). As with so much else in marriage, the whole key to getting yours into a good place is to stop looking around at what other couples are doing and focus solely on finding where you and your guy both feel comfortable and satisfied. "I finally figured out the number of times we need to have sex in order to keep us happy," one mom told us. "Anything more than two times a week is a task [for me], and anything less is not enough [for him]."

Let us repeat: That's great for *her*. What's normal for you and what works in your relationship is *not* necessarily the same as for everybody else. If other couples want to screw five times a week, or once a month, and they're happy that way, good for them. From our research we can tell you that nearly everybody questions whether they're getting or putting out more or less than their fair share. So do yourself a favor: Put the whole idea of comparing your sex life to other people's sex lives out of your mind. The only common trend we stumbled upon is that in families with young children, men tend to want to have more sex than their wives do.

DEAR GOD—PLEASE! I'M STILL ATTRACTED TO MY WIFE

"I miss her," one dad told us, echoing a lot of others. "The kids were gone this weekend . . . we actually had sex, but I had to convince her! Dear God—please! I'm still attracted to my wife. I would like to think she's still attracted to me. I've gotten gray, but not ugly!"

But even the idea that husbands want more sex than wives is not true across the board. "I feel like I'm the one who wants it more than he does, and it seems weird—most couples are the opposite," Gretchen confided. "We do talk about it. He's been going through stressful times with his family, and his energy level is low . . . at times I take that personally. If he can find time to surf the Web to look for

"It was really hard for me to consider myself a sexual being after Layla was born. That was really, really hard for me to overcome and get our sex lives back on track. It was brutal—it took six months of being really patient with each other."

SAMANTHA, married 3 years, 1 child, Brooklyn, NY

"My wife is the one who's dictating whether we have a good relationship or not. I believe that women have that control to turn it around. They have the say in whether or not you'll have sex. (That's the on or off button: Yes or no.) It's also the control of running the house, of running the kids—managing everything, including her intimate life."

RICK, married 10 years, 2 children, Sausalito, CA

cars, yet can't make time for sex, then it's hurtful. It's a self-esteem issue—I don't want to feel like I'm begging for it."

In couples with mismatched sex drives, part of the tension that arises is due to the sex itself (or the lack of it), and part is due to the fact that sex quickly becomes a proxy for how high up your spouse is on your priority list. Think about it: If sex is no more important than tidying up the house at the end of the day, or watching an episode of *American Idol*, or looking for cars on the Internet, that sends a big message to your significant other. As one mom, Beth, confessed, "I let my daughter suck every ounce out of me—and I don't give myself the breaks I need, and then I look at him in bed like 'forget it.' That would be the area to work on, and he would probably say he's less happy because of the lack of sex."

"I didn't get *nearly* enough sex when my kids were little, and I became very unsympathetic to my unfulfilled needs. I'm just waiting for the day that my last 18-year-old leaves the house so I can have more sex."

JACK, married 15 years, 3 children, Farmington, MI

"BOY, YOU'RE TIRED?" WHAT DOES THAT HAVE TO DO WITH ANYTHING?

A big component in sorting out sex in your marriage is figuring out how to deal with the fact that you and your husband are wired differently. Physiologically—hormonally—women change after giving birth. As Meg Newcomer, a family therapist, explains, "Research now shows that after the birth of two children, it affects the libido of women." In other words, when you brought that second newborn home from the hospital, your sex drive really did go down, while your husband's remained the same.

Another way to think about this is that we all have a hormonal "set point" that determines how high or low our sex drive is. For men, libido is mostly determined by testosterone level. Some men have high testosterone, and a lot of libido; some men have low testosterone and less libido. For women, it's both testosterone and estrogen levels. But interestingly, no matter what our natural set points, in the beginning of a romance our libido levels tend to match each other. Then they go back to "normal"—normal meaning your guy probably wants to have sex more than you do. "Nature gives your libido a boost in the early stages of love," Patricia Love and Steven Stosny write in *How to Improve Your Marriage Without Talking About It.* "But once that stage passes, you go back to your original set point." So at first you may think you're both on the same sexual playing field, but after the fireworks dim, you may not be as compatible as you thought.

However, pregnancy, childbirth, and (needless to say) children throw a big bucket of Legos on your bed. You feel bad about your body. You feel maxed out from nursing and neutralizing tantrums all day. Your husband, meanwhile, is having a different experience, and before you know it, your sexual desires and sexual needs begin to diverge. Maybe you start rebuffing some of his advances. He

DIRTY LITTLE SECRET

I have a number of times in my head that I have to have sex with my husband (two times per week) and if I don't meet it, I feel guilty. A lot of times it's just mercy sex.

naturally responds by feeling rejected. And that's how bad cycles start. Your natural feeling (not wanting to have sex when you're totally exhausted) becomes an affront (you're always exhausted, you never want to have sex). "I think guys are just so mechanical," one dad told us. "If you love your wife and you're content, you want to have sex. *'Boy, you're tired?'* What does that have to do with anything?' Guys are less emotional."

SHE WANTS FABIO SEX, HE WANTS PORN

Understanding how your chemistry differs from your husband's can make the situation less emotionally fraught, and that alone can help improve sex with your spouse. In *How to Improve Your Marriage Without Talking About It*, Patricia Love and Steven Stosny offer a little endocrinology lesson. "The hormones in a man's body that are responsible for arousal quickly build up and then are quickly released after orgasm. For a woman, the pleasure builds up much more slowly and remains long after orgasm." The authors go on to say, "The hidden reason a man is so much in a hurry to have sex is that through sex, a man is able to feel again. Sex helps him to feel again."

Just knowing this—that sex is a way for your husband to access his feelings—can also help soften the judgments we might feel of our spouse's needs. *(He wants to bonk even though we haven't had a real conversation in two weeks!?!)* Men often need sex in order to open up and communicate; women often need to have communicated first to want to have sex. But if you know that sex will help your husband connect with you more emotionally, you might feel more sympathetic

DIRTY LITTLE SECRET

Antidepressants might be the key to our happiness right now!

"It's not just sex. It's my way of connecting with her. I need that connection, which spills into raw emotions, which spills into everyday life. Intimacy is a major connection that we've lost. I knew the libido would be down on her end for a while. But it's never come back."

DENNIS, married 14 years, 2 children, Atlanta, GA

"We want two different kinds of sex. She wants emotional sex—slow, loving, Fabio with long hair and wind blowing and she's told she's loved the whole time. I want the physical sex, like in a porn magazine or in a film."

STAN, married 10 years, 2 children, Sioux Falls, SD

to his desire. As John Gray writes in *Mars and Venus in the Bedroom*, "It is through sex that a man's heart opens, allowing him to experience both his loving feelings and his hunger for love as well. Ironically, it is sex that allows a man to feel his needs for love, while it is receiving love that helps a woman to feel her hunger for sex."

"I just want to want my husband."

CLARA, married 12 years, 4 children, Madison, WI

IF WE WAIT FOR BOTH OF US TO BE IN THE MOOD, SEX WON'T EVER HAPPEN

All of this, of course, raises a very big question: How important is sex in marriage anyway?

The answer is *very*, but in a more complicated way than you might think. As Love and Stosny note, "Studies show that when things are going well, sex contributes only 15 percent to the overall satisfaction of a relationship. But if things aren't going well, it contributes 85 percent to the dissatisfaction. This is partly because a good sex life augments other areas of satisfaction so that it becomes one of many good things happening in the relationship."

DIRTY LITTLE SECRET

He works late—and so sometimes I will look at the clock and think he's coming home in a half hour and I scramble to get into bed real quick. And even if I hear him come in, I'm "fast asleep" suddenly.

Likewise, a bad sex life or a lack of sex life quickly spills over into other areas of your marriage.

If you want to improve things in your bedroom, being passive and waiting for the mood to strike is *not* the way to go. We heard this repeatedly from women we interviewed: They weren't really "in the mood" for sex (making them ultimately question how attracted they were to their spouses). But then once they were having sex, they enjoyed it. Afterward they'd even say to their husbands, "Wow, that was great—we should do that more often." Yet in the next day or two, or week, that feeling would literally evaporate. Interestingly, biology can help explain this pattern. "Most low-desire individuals do not feel the desire to have sex until they're highly aroused! You only want it when you're already doing it," write Love and Stosny. "In other words, you've got to do it to want it. This goes against everything we've been taught about sex."

The upshot is that while sex seems like something to do only when your impulses tell you it's time, a little jump-starting is valuable, particularly in a busy family life that doesn't include a lot of quiet, candlelit dinners. As one wife, Stacy, confirms, "If we wait for each of us to 'be in the mood,' then sex won't ever happen. We both need to sacrifice a little to get a lot."

The payoff is greater than it might seem at first. Everybody wants to be wanted. Not just that, we want to want our spouses, too. One important mind-shift to make is to stop seeing sex as just a physical thing. Sex is a measure and a reflection of how connected you and your spouse are to each other. A sex life is a fire that needs tending. If you don't, it'll just burn out. Researchers looking at hormones have also found that the more sex you have, the more you'll crave it. Just two weeks of no sex will lower your sex drive. Time to call the babysitter, huh?

Why
CAN HE TURN ANYTHING I SAY
INTO SOMETHING SEXUAL?

● ● ●

You: Can you go get the recycling out of the garage?

Him: Oh, I'll go in your garage any day!

You: Can you get us some cucumbers at the store?

Him: Oh, I got your cucumber right here, baby!

You: Can you pick up the dry cleaning after work?

Him: I'll dry clean *you*, baby!

You: That homework assignment was too hard.

Him: Oh, I'll give you hard.

You: How long was the flight?

Him: Oh, it was long, baby. *Real* long.

> "My mom told me if you don't give your guy sex, he will get it from someone else. Make a choice."
>
> CORY, married 7 years, 2 children, Pittsburgh, PA

PICK UP YOUR SOCKS IF YOU WANT TO HAVE SEX

The best place to start trying to heal your sex life is to realize that no matter what a horndog your husband might be, no matter how purely physical you think his desires are, sex (at least sex in marriage) is never just about sex. Sex with your spouse is about connecting on a deep and vulnerable level. What was your connection like when your romance began and you first started having sex? Spend some time with your spouse reminiscing. Chances are some good sex will come out of that!

It's also worth remembering that sex is a true investment in your marriage. Sex helps build a strong couple unit, and that unit is the foundation for your whole family. If we learned one thing from all our interviews, it was that we need to stop thinking of sex as yet another item on our to-do lists. That's really destructive for everybody: you, your spouse, and even your kids. Sex is vitally important. Would you so easily say no to something that nurtures so much love, intimacy, and trust?

"As a rule, I have never turned my shoulder away from him sexually—it's a really basic way to show appreciation and love. And once you get going, it's really great," Leigh confided in us. "Two-thirds he initiates and one-third I initiate. Last night he came home and I said, 'Yeah, I've been slinging mac and cheese, and I'm not in the mood!' but I came around and I had fun, eventually. I need a little more wind-up."

Guys, if you happen to be reading this, we want to give you a little tip: We heard endless stories from women who said watching their husbands do housework turned them on. For instance, "Pick up your socks if you want to have sex." Or "One night I was washing dishes in the kitchen at 11 P.M. and he hobbled over on his crutches asking, 'Can I do anything?' and he hopped up on the counter in desperation to help me . . . so that he could get me into bed!" It might not be anybody's fantasy vision of how a romantic marriage is supposed to work, but it sure does seem to do the trick! Jessica put out this plea: "If he helps me more around the house, I would do it every night. He just doesn't get it! All it takes is for him to clean the dishes to make me feel like he cares that it's important to me to have an organized household. I don't get angry if I have to ask, but I get really angry if he says no."

"God bless men, they're such simple creatures! Let's be honest—there are a *lot* of blow jobs right now! I hear you, you're a monkey, you need what you need. But you're not coming up in here at all!"

SHANA, married 4 years, 2 children, San Jose, CA

And gals, we heard just as many tales about women using sex as a tool to get what they want, often without their husbands even realizing what was going on. "He's really driven by sex," Jennie told us. "I'm not a hornball like he is. [Yet] I notice that when I offer it up, he'll be really happy with me for the rest of the day."

The small touches in life also seem to go a very long way toward keeping a physical connection alive, both in addition to sex and in lieu of sex if for whatever reason—too pregnant, too soon after a baby—sex just isn't happening in your world right now. Men are often much more desirous of feeling loved and wanted than their wives realize. Little touches like telling him he's handsome, or he smells nice, or that you still love the sound of his voice, can go a very long way. Same with daily rituals, like kissing him goodbye on the mouth, or holding hands in the car. "Feeling connected and loved and wanted isn't about sex," says one dad we talked to, Rod. "You can hire hookers for sex. But kissing someone, and hugging someone and squeezing their ass when they walk by . . . *that* will lead to awesome sex."

"I feel like we can just check in with each other easily and feel connected, while we're standing there doing dishes. It's daily little things for us."

JEMMA, married 10 years, 3 children, Santa Barbara, CA

GETTING AWAY FROM THE HOUSE PRETTY MUCH GUARANTEES SEX

So, should you go pick him up at the train station naked under your raincoat? Different couples offered up different tricks for keeping the conjugal bliss alive. One mom we spoke to shared with us what she and her husband call "the wink." When one of them wants sex that night, they wink at each other across the room, and it builds anticipation and excitement, knowing that one of them wants the other. "Especially during times when there's a thousand kids running around and the neighbors are over; we give each other the wink if we want to have sex. And maybe later on or in the next day or two we might actually 'meet up' with each other."

Other parents told us they swore by getting away from their normal routine for a night or two every month. Just breaking out of the characters of "mom" and "dad" can really help revive that physical connection you last felt on the plane ride home from your honeymoon. Some couples manage to do this at home; others get more literal and skip off to a hotel. "My husband and I went on a vacation alone for our tenth anniversary, and it was shocking how much that reignited our sex life," said one mom named Angela. "For the first time in years since having kids, we saw each other in a sexual way, with all of the elements removed—financial, house, kid, and job pressures. I felt like me again—and it was an amazing feeling. Even now, back in our daily routine, all I have to do is know that somewhere inside, we have the ability to get that spark back."

Every couple needs to figure out what will work for them now, in this stage of their lives, and not endlessly bemoan the loss of the early days, when you wanted each other so much you made love in bathrooms and cars. Redefine what a good sex life means now that you're . . . you. And then work like hell to fan those flames. As always, nothing is silly or clichéd or out of bounds. Not even a dirty weekend in Las Vegas. As Rachel told us, "I've had this fascination with Vegas, and we've gone twice since the boys have been born. And

DIRTY LITTLE SECRET

My husband would kill me if he knew this, but I check e-mail on my Blackberry while I'm driving my kids around in the car.

it's been *great* for our sex life! Getting away from the house pretty much guarantees sex. But in the house, when the boys are there, forget it. I put the red light on, but he is not instigating either. The last thing I really want is anybody to touch me."

"The more acts of kindness you give me around this house that benefit me—the more likely that I will be in the mood. The more you do, the more we'll screw."

BETH, married 5 years, I child, Seattle, WA

WHAT I WISH SHE KNEW . . .

○ "I wish she knew how hard I work and how little appreciation I feel."

○ "I wish we could have a little more of what we were, again, someday."

○ "I wish my wife knew she is still hot. Even with the smell of spit-up."

○ "I wish my wife knew I can only do my job because she does hers."

○ "I wish she knew how hard it is to live on two hours' less sleep than her every day!"

steps
for reigniting the fire

1. Remember that what's normal for you is unique to you as a couple. If having sex once every three weeks or three days is agreeable to both of you, then that is OK. Although we know it's hard to talk about, just simply understanding each other's needs can make a world of difference.

2. Realize that you may just be in a phase. Having a newborn or feeling a lot of stress can put a strain on your sex life. (At the same time, be aware when a phase is lasting too long. It can turn into a negative pattern.)

3. Focus your attention on what you like about your partner (and verbalize it!). Sometimes, just stepping out of the day-to-day stress and remembering something positive about your spouse can work wonders.

4. If you're in a rut, one mom recommended having sex every day for one week to force yourself into a new routine and remind yourself that you actually like sex—and your husband. Or for one week, no one is allowed to say no to any kind of advances.

5. You could also decide together that for one week, you'll just kiss and hug, and not have sex. Some women told us they even started to fear cuddling and kissing because they worried it would lead to sex.

6. Or, commit to the number of times you will have sex for a given period (for example, certain days of the week or once a week for a month). That way one of you won't feel rejected and the other won't stress about being pawed.

7. Carve out time for each other without feeling guilty about the kids. If you need to put it on the calendar, fine. That's better than it not happening at all.

8. For a sure bet, there's always the purple rabbit (but you didn't hear this from us).

CHAPTER 7

WHERE
do we go
FROM HERE?

. . .

So, gals, where are we? IF
YOU'RE ANYTHING LIKE US, BETWEEN THE TIME YOU STARTED
THIS BOOK AND YOU FINISHED IT, NOT ALL THAT MUCH
has changed. You're still a mom, you're still a wife, your children
still interfere with 98 percent of your attempts to create peace and
romance in your life, and your husband, God bless him, still doesn't
have any relationship to the hamper—let alone the washing machine.

But you want to stay married and you want to enjoy it—and you
do love your husband—so you need to make a commitment to yourself to consciously *work* at creating happiness in your marriage.

We've all heard it before—marriage is work. There's no way
around that. But you can control the kind of work you're doing.
You can control what you're working toward. Do you really want to
just suck it up for fifty stressful years? Work at keeping your temper
from flaring over when he's bald and you're both wrinkled and he
still doesn't know how to put his shoes away? We'd all rather work
at creating joy and union in our marriages—at supporting each other,
fanning the flames of our romances, and reaping the benefits of lives
spent truly known and loved by each other.

If you take a step back and look at it rationally, marriage is crazy. You pin your heart, your dreams, your finances, your home, your children, and your vacations to this one person. What, are you nuts?! Yet life is funny. We fall in love, we dream of getting married, we walk down the aisle (or up the courthouse steps), and commit to this other person to stay together until parted by death. So let us be clear: We're not out to question the institution of marriage. (We'll leave that to more radical thinkers than ourselves.) Our aim is to simply look at how we're defining what a good marriage is. To question the assumptions and expectations we've brought to our married lives. It's because we believe so deeply in marriage, and are so committed to avoiding divorce, that we're so insistent on being honest about matrimony. Really, after putting so much stock in one person—your emotional life, your material life, your offspring—who in her right mind would be passive about whether or not she's happy in her marriage? Who would let herself get derailed by the illusion of a perfect marriage? To us, that's the crazy part.

Creating your own happiness in marriage is not as tricky as it might seem. Half the battle is rejiggering the images in our heads. If you expected every day to begin and end with an epic *From Here to Eternity* kiss, you're probably feeling pretty disappointed with your husband just about now. But if we had to guess, 90 percent of the problem is not your marriage—it's your expectations. We owe it to ourselves—and our husbands, and our kids—to weigh the reality of our marriages against realistic standards. One of our favorite guilty

DIRTY LITTLE SECRET

He was so good with the dogs and attentive to them and I just presumed that he would be good with babies. Uh . . . not so much.

pleasures is reading *Star* magazine in the grocery checkout line. It's a great reminder: Everything in Hollywood, especially Hollywood marriages, is not what it seems.

We also believe that it's up to us to be proactive about the moods that permeate our homes. Moods might seem like weather, but they're actually much more malleable than we think. We have the power to make a happy environment or a stressed-out one. Sure, your husband might come home exhausted, barking, pissed at his boss. And while you can't do much about the mood he brings through the door, you *can* control how you handle the situation. We can either create tension and chaos, or create peace, in moments small and large, in our marriages every day.

The choice is up to you.

Keeping perspective on the size of certain transgressions can also go a long way toward fostering good feelings in your home. Sure, the bills need to be paid, your in-laws drive you crazy, and how could anybody possibly keep her cool with a toddler banging on the freezer door demanding a Popsicle before breakfast while the phone is ringing every ten minutes? But the truth is we never know what the future holds, good or bad. The only thing that's for sure is that in what will seem like ten minutes, our kids will be gone, off living their lives. All we have is right now. Accepting and enjoying what we've got is the biggest gift we can give our families and ourselves.

The vast majority of mothers we spoke to told us they were better at seizing the moment with their kids than with their spouses. Children's needs are urgent—and even if they're not, they're often presented that way—so it's not surprising that kids have entrenched themselves in the number-one spot on our priority lists. But our husbands crave our attention, too—and we crave theirs, often more than we let ourselves realize. The best mother is not the mother who suffers and sacrifices the most. The best mother is the one who can give and receive love and teach her children how to go out and find love for themselves in the world. After all, the goal of being a parent is to raise your children to be independent, to leave you and have their own lives in the world. And that leaves a mother and father once again on their own, alone as a couple. Your marriage needs to be nurtured and tended, just like your kids.

So for goodness sake, give yourself permission to leave the laundry unfolded and the work e-mails unanswered, and sit down with your husband after the kids are asleep and have a *conversation* with him. Our guess is that it will turn into the most important twenty minutes in your day. You can't sustain a relationship on a once-a-month date night. A daily connection is vital for the longevity—and happiness—of a marriage.

This is not just a personal issue, it's a family one. How we talk to each other, how we fight, how we portray marriage, even how we communicate nonverbally affects our kids. Showing them and telling them that no marriage is perfect, but ours is good nonetheless, is a crucial message for their future success. If your kids hear each of you saying "thank you" and "I love you" to each other, they'll expect the same in their own relationships as adults. (Let's not even talk about their relationships as teenagers!) Even the parts of your marriage that seem to be for your benefit alone—sex, dates, weekends away—aren't as adult-centered as they might seem. When you and your husband go out for the night or away for a few days, and you explain to your children that "we need this to stay connected, to be good parents for you, and to strengthen the family," that's an important lesson for them. We're shaping our kids' visions of what a caring, committed relationship with children looks like, and if nothing else, we need to prioritize our marriage for them to see. Part of being a mature adult is knowing how to take care of yourself. Your children need to see examples. Besides, if you and your husband are in sync and well connected, you'll be better people and better parents, a more solid core of a more solid family unit.

Counterintuitively, in addition to being together, you also need to allow each other to grow individually. The goal of a happy marriage isn't to shackle your spouse to your side, or force him to remain the same person he was when you two walked down the aisle. Allowing each other to grow—and grow organically—is as important as maintaining your bond. Change, particularly change in a spouse, can be scary and confusing. (Wait a minute—I didn't marry a guy who was obsessed with flamenco guitar!) But if we're going to stay together for the long haul, we need to let each other grow. We need to support each other, whether a spouse is learning a new sport, trying to change careers, or going on a spiritual journey, and we need to demand that he does the same for us. Over the years, we will change—we must change, or we'll stagnate and grow bored. Marriage is a journey— a long one. Would you rather go down the road for a thousand unknown miles, or would you rather do five hundred laps around the same small two-mile track?

Viewing the whole messy picture of marriage and family life through a positive lens is not always easy to do, and it certainly is not easy to maintain. But a commitment to it can be the catalyst for a far happier existence. If you're in a good space in your marriage, nourish it, cherish it, appreciate it—encourage the goodness to grow. If you're in a so-so place (the vast majority of you who told us you were a 5 or 6 on the 10-point happiness scale), look for what's good, and nurture, cherish, and appreciate that—chances are

DIRTY LITTLE SECRET

You can sleep with my husband before you take my babysitter!

it will rub off on the rest. And if you're in a not-so-great place, focus on the elements—even just one element—worth appreciating right now. Commit yourself to sustaining that piece, and use it to lay the groundwork for more peace and happiness in your home.

No marriage is perfect. Not ours, not yours, not anybody's we spoke to. So let yourself off the hook. Don't mourn the loss of fireworks. Don't pity yourself for the small skirmishes that fill your days. The best thing you can do for your marriage is to clear out all the thoughts in your head of what a good marriage is supposed to look like, and spend some time with your spouse defining what a good marriage means for you. Happiness will not arrive on schedule just because you marked it on the calendar for 2021, or whatever the year will be when you kids leave the house. Happiness is waiting for you today. You just need to go out and work toward it—toward that happy marriage and happy life that you deserve.

DIRTY LITTLE SECRET

We lied to our husbands and told them we were starting our own book group—but really we'd meet in a bar!

"There are days I would trade my husband for just about anything, and then there are days I wouldn't trade him for anything—like this morning when he finally coaxed Abby into an outfit after all my mommy maneuverings failed to help her find an outfit appropriate for school that also satisfied her need for fashion! He deserves a daddy raise this morning!"

CASSIE, married 8 years, 2 children, Kentfield, CA

Acknowledgments

Thank you to all the moms and dads we interviewed. Without your honesty we wouldn't be able to learn so much from each other. Paul, thank you for cherishing what we've built together, and for knowing what matters most. You are my love, my life. Eric, thank you for making it so easy to love you, and always believing in our love. You are simply the true love of my life and I feel blessed every day. To our children, Alex, Pierce, Julia, Sam, and Emily, we look forward to witnessing the discovery of pure love in your lives. Kathy and Peter Nobile, your very real, very beautiful marriage continues to be an inspiration. Phyllis Menken, you've always believed in me, no matter what—thank you. Val and Jerry Gibbons, you've shown me that true love lasts forever, and a strong marriage can be the most empowering tool in life. Thank you for that gift. Nancy and Larry Ashworth, thank you for continuing to show us that marriage is a true partnership. You make it look easy. Sarah Malarkey, for your continued support and open mind. Jodi Warshaw, thank you for your patience and complete faith in our vision. Jennifer Tolo Pierce—once again, perfection! Nancy Deane and Christina Loff, thank you for your rock star efforts each and every day. Elizabeth Weil—your talent is extraordinary. Abby Hoffman, thank you and thank you again. Barry Schwartz, Meg Newcomer, Pat Covalt, Christine Ryan, Joshua Coleman, Kim Bellisimo—thank you for your knowledge and expertise. Shelley Mosby, for celebrating everything as though it was the first time and redefining what "best friend" means, I love you. Nora Clifford and Keira Muller—your rock-solid support and friendship is something for which I am truly grateful. Susan Maher, you're precious to me, no matter how close or far. Rose Wells—we both love you to pieces. Tracy Brennan and Millie Froeb, thank you for your generous hearts, kind spirits, and for being the true best friends that you are. Marcia Rozelle and Marsha Austen, thank you for many years of insight and perspective. I am grateful to have you both in my life. Mindy Mutscheller, you have the biggest heart. I am lucky to know you. Thank you to our families, including: Scott Gibbons, Cristin Gibbons, Linly and Gary Belshaw, Carie and Rick Betram, Cheryl and Michael Nobile, Jan Power and Peter Nobile, Beth Babini, and Evan Menken. Thank you Eddie's and Café Marmalade for keeping us full and happy. And of course a continued thank you to our friends who drive our positive energy: Kara Clanton, Brooke Anderson, Jodi Bricker, Miranda Abrams, Lindsay Walsh, Andrea Fohrman, Hannah Hudson, Annie Bjork, Debi Roche, Amy Finn, Andrea Rothschild, Victoria Maitland, Gracy Wooster, Rachel and Mark Klein, Rachel Fisch, Tami Anderson, Christy Salcido, Mark Malinowski, Brian Ades, Steve Josoma, Peter Dominguez, Ron and Kim Vandenberg, Aaron Mutscheller, Mike Roche, Doreen Cortell, Lisa Kuhn, Laurie Brants, John Bonasso, Claudine and Dan Osipow, Nancy Ludwick, Ashley Ray, Jackie Cisne, Regina Voorhis, Vali and Curtis Nemetz, Steve and Grace Cabalka, Ginny Weichert, Diane Blake, Jesse Ludwick, Mary Lasher, Kathy Heath, Julie Thomson, Kailey Lewis, Merrill Slaugh, Janell Hobart, and Marcy Grantor.